To Anne & Whit,

Best wishes

Jim Rossi

DINO ROSSI:
LESSONS IN LEADERSHIP, BUSINESS, POLITICS, AND LIFE

DINO ROSSI

Forward ▶ Books

Forward Books LLC
15100 SE 38th ST #787
Bellevue • WA • 98006
PH • 425-653-1582
www.forwardbooks.com

10 9 8 7 6 5 4 3 2

Printed in the United States of America

LCCN 2005935234
ISBN 0-9773262-0-9

Editor: Vicki McCown
Jacket Design and Photography: Daniel MacLeod/PromoLab
Interior Layout: Stephanie Martindale

DEDICATION

To Terry, my wonderful wife. Eighteen years and four beautiful children later, I'm still the luckiest guy on earth. To Juliauna, Jake, Joseph and little Jillian. I'm proud of you all.

CONTENTS

ACKNOWLEDGMENTS

I have been blessed throughout my life with people who helped me get to where I am today. There are too many friends & mentors who can never be thanked enough.

It starts with my late and very much missed parents, John and Eve Rossi. They gave me the foundation and guidance I needed to make my way in the world.

My brothers and sisters, Jessica, Margie, Duncan, Dick, Bill, and my late brother Bill, all taught me many valuable lessons in life. (Yes I have two brothers named Bill, but that's a story for another day.)

There is no way to adequately thank the following people: Afton Swift, J. Vanderstoep, Mary Lane, Ryan Moore, Brian Smith and Chris Widener. I am eternally grateful for your friendship and assistance with this book.

Thank you to all the people throughout my life who gave me a chance to prove myself.

Thank you to the people of the state of Washington for your faith in me.

Above all, I would like to thank God for all the blessings He has bestowed upon me.

INTRODUCTION

When I ran for governor of Washington in 2004, I spent twelve months criss-crossing the state, meeting thousands of people, listening to their concerns and sharing my vision for what our state could become. As most of you know, I won the first vote and the first recount and lost the second recount. But with all the serious irregularities we observed in the election—mainly in King County, the largest county in Washington—the state Republican Party decided to file an election challenge in the state Superior Court. In June 2005, we lost the challenge.

Throughout the election I said I'd be happy whether I was in politics or not, and I meant it. In the months since the court challenge ended, I've spent most of my time with my family—including a cross-country road trip with one of my sons—and have also been able to dedicate more hours to my favorite pastime, golf, as well as to my commercial real estate business. After some reflection and conversations with colleagues, friends and family, I also decided that now was a good time to set down my thoughts about my life so far in the context of a book on leadership.

I never wanted to write a book just for the sake of writing a book; instead, I wanted to share my experiences on what I've learned about life, business and politics, and in the process perhaps help people in their own lives. During the gubernatorial campaign, I figure I talked first-hand to about 50,000 people. I found that people responded when I talked about issues and related them to my own experiences. Even in those many speeches, however, my time was limited and I wasn't able to share many stories of the people and events that shaped me as a young man and helped me become the person I am today. It was fun and rewarding to recollect those stories as I wrote this book.

You'll notice as you read the book that I've asked a friend of mine to contribute his thoughts at the end of each chapter. Chris Widener has been my friend since before I entered politics, and he spent a lot of time with me on the campaign trail. Chris is a nationally recognized speaker and author on the topics of leadership, motivation and personal development. I asked Chris to highlight the basic principle of each chapter and write a "life application" summary to help you think about how the principle can work in your life.

I hope you enjoy the stories of my life as much as I enjoyed writing them down. I also hope that when you read them, you realize that the principles of a successful life are universal and can be lived by anyone. Whether you are in politics, business, a parent, a schoolteacher, or in a non-profit organization, the principles

I share in this book apply to situations and challenges many of you face on a daily basis. A positive attitude, perseverance, leadership, integrity and courage are themes of my life, and I believe they can be helpful to you as well.

Finally, I'd like to thank everyone who has been so supportive over the past few years. My family and I have been blessed by the friendship we share with so many wonderful people.

Enjoy!

Dino Rossi

Chapter One

STAY TRUE TO WHO YOU ARE!

People will follow a leader who sticks to his or her principles and values, who is consistent in his or her beliefs and behavior, regardless of what may be politically correct or expedient. This doesn't mean people have to agree with that leader on all things. In fact, an effective leader welcomes dialogue on an issue. It also doesn't mean a leader must be rigid; given new information or innovative ideas, good leaders can change their point of view or even admit a mistake. A leader people will follow is someone who is honest and straightforward and who exhibits a strong character worthy of their trust, no matter how difficult a situation may be.

I have often spoken before groups of people I knew held an opposing point of view to mine. Whenever I find myself in that position—and what elected official doesn't?—I tell my audience what I believe, but always in a way that respects their beliefs. In short, I find a way to disagree without being disagreeable.

Once during my campaign for governor in 2004 I found myself speaking before a group I knew wasn't going to be thrilled with a couple of my proposals. I took the direct approach.

"You probably aren't going to like this one," I said, and then proceeded to tell them the truth about a difficult issue facing our state, what I felt needed to be done, and how to do it. As I spoke, I could see a few frowns in the audience.

"Listen," I concluded, "we aren't going to agree 100 percent of the time. But, hey, I bet you don't agree with your own spouse 100 percent of the time, and I'm not asking you to marry me."

The laugh I got told me my audience appreciated my frankness, even if some of them didn't see things my way. I ended up getting the support of many of the people in the room that night, because I treated them with honesty as well as courtesy.

Leaders speak straight from the heart and mean what they say, which is one main reason why people follow them. Nobody wants to put their trust in a person who would say or do anything to succeed. You never really know where that person stands on an issue, let alone where he or she will lead you.

In my first state Senate race in 1992, I competed for a seat representing a brand-new, incumbent-free district created by redistricting. Many Republicans surfaced to vie for that seat, and I found myself facing three challengers for the party nomination. Before the primary, the Republican Senate Campaign Committee summoned all four of us for a sort of glorified "dog and pony show." They wanted to check us out, to see if any of us merited their support.

Dino's father John Rossi

Dino's mother Eve Rossi

During the discussion, I noticed one of the senators staring at the piece of paper that listed our names. After some time, he looked up at me and asked, "Have you ever thought about changing your name to 'Dean Ross'?" Apparently, he thought that by making my name more mainstream and less ethnic, I might get a few more votes.

I shook my head. "You know, my mom and dad gave me this name," I said. "I'm not Dean Ross; I'm Dino Rossi." Then I looked him square in the eye, holding his gaze. "I don't believe having an unusual name hurt State Senator Emilio Cantu." (Emilio is a former member of the state senate and one of my political mentors.)

He flushed and I could see I had made my point. I wasn't some film star who needed a more marketable name to further my career. I liked my name, and I wanted people to know me for who I really was. I refused to deny my heritage just to become a senator.

🙣

Our heritage is part of what shapes us as individuals, what helps us define and develop our values. My own heritage is varied, colorful, and filled with difficult lessons.

My grandfather, Silvino Rossi, immigrated to this country around the turn of the twentieth century. Silvino came from the little Italian country town of Taranta Peligna, about a four-hour drive from Rome. He originally settled in New York, where he met and married my grandmother, Concetta. But in the cement jungle that is New York City, Silvino missed the trees, the fields, the blue sky he grew up with in Italy. Most of all, he missed

Grandpa Silvino Rossi's home town, Taranta Peligna, Italy

The Catholic Church in Taranta Peligna

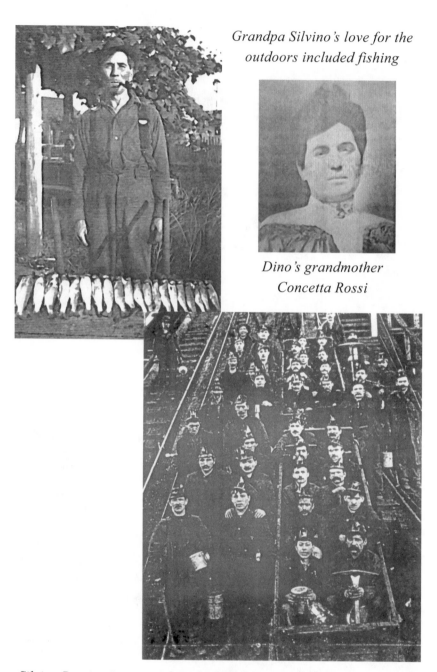

Grandpa Silvino's love for the outdoors included fishing

Dino's grandmother Concetta Rossi

Silvino Rossi going to work in the Black Diamond coal mines. Silvino is in the back on the far left and appears to be the only one smiling

having a river to fish in like the one that flowed through his village. Eventually my grandparents made their way across the country to Washington, where my grandfather had family in the rural community of Black Diamond, about 35 miles southeast of Seattle.

One of the few jobs an Italian could land at that time was working in the coal mines—strenuous, dangerous work that paid just a few dollars a day. But my grandfather was proud of the work he did. Through honest labor, he could feed and clothe his family. If you visit the Black Diamond Museum today, you will see the two-man saw he used back in those days. Hard work, taking pride in caring for one's family—this is part of my heritage that comes from Grandpa Silvino.

Silvino passed on his love of the outdoors to my father, who passed it on to my siblings and me. When my wife Terry and I visited my grandfather's home town in Italy on our honeymoon, we understood Silvino's passion. In Taranta Peligna, we found a pristine village sitting on the banks of a beautiful river—it would be impossible not to love nature and its beauty coming from such a spot. An appreciation of the outdoors—this, too, is my heritage. It's also part of the heritage of the people of Washington State and one of the reasons I made restoration of our state parks system one of the main issues in my gubernatorial campaign.

While my father's side of the family is all Italian, my mother's side is a bit more mixed. About the same time Silvino emigrated from Italy, my Irish grandfather on my mother's side, Patrick McClusky, set out for Alaska in search of gold. He married my grandmother, Mary, an Alaska native of the Tlingit tribe.

Dino's grandmother Mary McClusky in Klawock, Alaska (1920)

The Rossi Family - Black Diamond, Washington (1914)

Shortly after my mother was born, my grandfather died—under circumstances that still remain hazy. My grandmother became a single mom (although she later remarried) and my own mother grew up in near poverty. This is my heritage too.

I often get asked, "What kind of Republican are you?" People try to place me in a certain type of political box, one that's convenient or understandable. But my answer usually throws them.

"I am a part Tlingit, part Irish, half Italian, Catholic Republican who comes from a conservative Democrat family." Understandably, many people aren't quite sure what to make of that. Perhaps the part that throws them the most is the "Democrat" part of the equation.

> "I am a part Tlingit, (Alaskan native) part Irish, half Italian, Catholic Republican who comes from a conservative Democrat family."

It's true. My family's political history has been more Democrat than Republican. I think of my father as a "Scoop Jackson" kind of conservative Democrat— someone who followed his own conscience and principles and could think for himself. (Henry "Scoop" Jackson was a longtime and nationally renowned conservative Democratic U.S. Senator from the state of Washington.)

I remember the first opportunity I had to vote for president. It was 1980 and Republican Ronald Reagan was challenging the incumbent president, Democrat Jimmy Carter. Like I said, I came from a Democrat-leaning family, but the person who steered me toward becoming a Republican the most was Jimmy Carter himself. While Jimmy Carter seemed like a nice man, and I'm sure he would have been a great guy to have as, say, an uncle or a friend, I couldn't help thinking he didn't seem like the kind of leader our country needed. In comparing Ronald Reagan to President Carter, I could see a tremendous difference. Where Carter offered no hope for our future, suggesting America suffered from a national malaise, Reagan exuded unbridled optimism about America's future, which he backed up with policies he planned to implement, such as strengthening our national defense.

At the time of the 1980 election, I was a student in the School of Business at Seattle University. As someone who had been a "business person" since the age of seven, the entrepreneurial aspects of the Republican Party attracted me. I saw the Republicans as the party that tried to marry support of the free enterprise system with the idea of creating across-the-board economic opportunities, so that everyone had a chance to be successful. This same set of ideals keeps me a Republican today.

I voted for Ronald Reagan in the 1980 presidential election, and I felt confident about my choice. However, I knew at home that evening we'd talk about the election, and I wasn't sure how my dad would feel about the choice I'd made in the voting booth.

I started the conversation.

"I voted today, Dad."

"Glad to hear you did," he said with a smile. "Do you want to tell me who you voted for?"

"Ronald Reagan," I said, hoping I sounded as confident as I felt. I looked at my dad, the man I loved and respected, and wondered whether he would question my vote.

But I was in for a surprise.

"So did I," he said.

Ronald Reagan, a former Democrat, once said he hadn't left the Democratic Party; the Democratic Party had left him. I know many fellow Republicans who feel the same way. Evidently my dad was one of them. This, too, is part of my heritage.

#

A valuable lesson I learned from my grandparents and my parents is that I must always be true to myself. This isn't always easy, especially when doing so means I might lose something I value, such as a friend.

Skip Rowley has been a friend and supporter of mine since my first run for public office in 1992. Skip and I agree on many issues, which is probably why we clicked the first time we met. In Issaquah, Washington (just outside of Seattle), Skip is known as that proverbial "pillar of the community." He has served on numerous city boards and commissions. He is always one of the first to help when the community is in trouble. Not only has Skip been a good friend, he has been one of my mentors, someone I can always count on. Every community should be so lucky as to have a generous, civic-minded citizen like Skip Rowley.

But, as much as I like and respect Skip and see eye-to-eye with him on most issues, there have been times when I had to tell him I felt differently than he did. One such instance occurred in 1997 shortly after I was elected as state senator.

Skip showed up unexpectedly one day in my Senate office; he had come to try and convince me to vote for a gas tax increase. I looked at my friend, this wonderful guy and community leader—not to mention one of my biggest supporters—and gave him an apologetic smile.

"Skip, what did I do during the campaign that led you to believe I would vote for a gas tax increase?" I asked. When I saw his surprise, I explained that I had to be a "no" vote until I saw more efficiency in the transportation budget, as well as a way to tie the allocation of funds to specific projects instead of just throwing money around the state.

I could see Skip was not only disappointed in me, but frustrated by my point of view. While there were many transportation projects both Skip and I wanted to see completed, I felt we weren't using the funds we already had as efficiently as we should have been. In fact, as I write this book, I believe we still don't prioritize new projects with congestion relief in mind. I refused to vote for the gas tax increase in 1997 until I was satisfied the taxpayers' money was being spent wisely.

It took courage to say no to a friend and one of my staunchest supporters. Seeing he couldn't sway me, Skip went back home, and I worried that maybe this would be the end of our relationship. That prospect saddened me. But, as much as I would hate losing Skip as a friend, I felt even more strongly that I had to stick to my principles and to what I had promised on the campaign trail.

After the session ended and I returned home, one of the first things I did was to make an appointment to see Skip. When we met, he told me that, although he was disappointed in my "no" vote on the gas tax, he also found what I had done to be refreshing.

"I've told a lot of people in town how I went down to Olympia looking for a 'yes' vote on the gas tax," he said. "But instead I found something quite remarkable: an elected official who does what he says he's going to do." In the end, Skip was actually proud of me. Even though he didn't get what he wanted, he respected my commitment to honoring my word. I'm happy to say that Skip and I have a great friendship that continues today.

⁕

During the campaign for governor of Washington, I took part in a televised debate with another gubernatorial hopeful, Democratic King County Executive Ron Sims, which was broadcast statewide. One question was about abortion.

The question came to me first.

"I'm not running for the U.S. Supreme Court," I answered, "and in the seven years I've spent in the Senate, I have never sponsored a bill concerning that issue. However, it is an issue I feel strongly about. My wife Terry and I are both Catholic, and we believe that every soul has a value. This belief is one of the reasons I fought so hard in the budget for the mentally ill and the developmentally disabled. In my mind, every soul is worth protecting."

In Washington State, where I believe at least 60 percent of citizens would say they are pro-choice to one degree or another, many saw my point of view on this as a political liability. In fact, some of my supporters had suggested that I change my position.

"You know, Dino, this really isn't an issue for the governor," they argued. "Why don't you just change your position? If you do, you'll be a shoo-in."

While I know they believed they were giving me good advice, I simply couldn't follow it.

As I stood facing the cameras that evening of the debate, I knew I had to be clear on this issue, that what I said at this moment would help define who I was to the Washington voters.

"No matter what side of the issue you are on, abortion is an issue of conscience," I said. "If I have to change my position on an issue of conscience just to be elected governor, I would rather not be governor."

You could have heard a pin drop in that television studio.

The feedback I received after that debate was enlightening—especially the reaction from those people who didn't agree with me. Even though they might argue against my point of view, they respected my answer. Here was a guy running for governor who would rather not win if it meant violating his conscience. Unbelievable!

Suddenly, people who didn't agree with me and who perhaps might not have supported me before were now going to vote for me—all because of that answer. Why? Because I spoke from the heart and I was true to my beliefs. I didn't flinch, or put a softer spin on what I thought, or change my position just to make me more attractive to certain groups in the hope of gaining their vote.

Throughout the entire campaign for governor, I played it straight with the public. I didn't bother to slant my views one way for some groups, then a different way for others. When you rely on that kind of strategy, it's too difficult to remember what you promised and to whom. I figured I'd just be myself; if people liked me and agreed with what I had to say, that'd be great. If they didn't, that would be okay too. I had other things I could do with my life.

While serving as a senator, I've witnessed elected officials who seem to have their insides twisting on every single vote. It always made me wonder how they conducted their campaign. Did they have one position at the Kiwanis and a different position at the Rotary? Are they devoid of principles to guide them or do they simply want to please everyone?

This rudderless style of "leadership" is, in fact, not leadership at all. Great leaders remain true to themselves, their ideals, their principles. And because they do so, they inspire others to follow.

Be true to yourself...and if others follow, they will do so for the right reasons. That is a credo for leaders to live by.

KEY PRINCIPLE

Always Live By Your Values and Principles

There is absolutely nothing worth compromising your principles. Nothing. When all is said and done, all we have left are our core values and principles. If we betray them, we betray ourselves. We make ourselves weaker and become hollow leaders.

Why is it that people betray their values and principles? We're all tempted to do so at one point or another, aren't we? This betrayal is the result of our perception of a personal short-term expediency. We think that, in the short term, short-changing our values will be beneficial to us. What we don't realize in our cloudy thinking is that, regardless of the pressure we feel to conform or the so-called "positive benefit" we may receive, in the long run our actions chip away at our ethical foundation and ruin our long-term potential for success by betraying our core values.

Dino mentioned Skip Rowley. I also know Skip and he is one of the great businessmen and leaders in our area, well-respected by just about everyone I know. With that in mind, I can see how it would be difficult to stand your ground on your ideas and principles when someone like Skip thinks you are wrong. However, Dino did just that, and because he stayed true to his principles, we now have two strong and respected leaders – Dino *and* Skip.

Do you feel pressure to compromise your principles? What are you doing to make sure you don't succumb? If you are feeling pressure to betray your core values and principles, one of the best things you can do is to find a partner who can help you weather the storm. Ask that person for help and support. Ask him or her for encouragement. And then, each time you are confronted with pressure to compromise, take the time to think clearly and make the right choice to stay true to who you are.

◡ Chris Widener

Chapter 2

MY PATH TO BECOMING A BUSINESSMAN

When it came time for me to go to college, I gave careful consideration to what career I wanted to pursue. My father was a public school elementary teacher, and I admired both him and his profession. I decided that would be a great career for me too.

I went to my father and said, "Dad, I've been thinking about what I should study in college, what career path I should follow. I think I would like to follow in your footsteps—to be a schoolteacher just like you."

I thought he would be proud of my choice, pleased that I wanted to follow the same profession he had chosen.

But he had different ideas.

"Dino," he said, giving me a penetrating look, "you have been a businessman since you were seven. You have a gift. I've watched it grow and develop over the years. It would be a shame not to nurture that inherent talent. I think you should go to business school. You can always come back to teaching—and

Dino's fatherJohn Rossi, a Seattle Public school teacher,
with one of his 5th grade classes.

probably whenever you want to and on your own terms. Go into the business world, implement your ideas, make your money. That's where you belong."

My dad didn't give a lot of advice, but when he did I listened. I entered the Seattle University School of Business.

❦

When I was three years old, the Rossi family moved from the Seattle neighborhood near the Woodland Park Zoo north to Mountlake Terrace in Snohomish County. It was a great place to grow up. Our neighbors had horses, chickens, and cows. The kids in the neighborhood spent most summers playing in the acres and acres of woods near our home. My friends and I would ride bikes, go fishing, and play baseball from dawn to dusk.

On one of my summer bike trips I ended up at Ballinger Park Golf course, a little nine-hole golf course on Lake Ballinger in south Snohomish County. I noticed that most of the left side of hole #8 was covered with sticker bushes, and buried in those bushes were golf balls. I knew if I tried to retrieve them, all I'd get were a bunch of bloody scratches. But I had an idea.

The next day I rode back to the golf course wearing my heavy winter coat. People must have thought I was crazy, standing out on the golf course, dressed for the deep of winter on what was a beautiful 80-degree summer's day. I didn't care. One pass through the sticker bushes produced three dozen golf balls. I went back to the tee and sold those golf balls to the guys teeing off.

And a businessman was born.

I began retrieving the golf balls on a regular schedule and sales were brisk. At seven years old, I was making as much as $30 a weekend. It was a good little business that helped me to learn how to sell.

When I was in junior high school, a kid at school brought in some candles he'd made as a hobby. I was intrigued, thinking this might be a fun way to make some money. But, to go into business, I would need some investment capital. I went to my dad.

"Dad, could I borrow some money?" I said. "I'd like to start a candle-making business."

"A candle-making business," he repeated, probably wondering where the heck I'd gotten such an impractical idea. "Just how much do you need?"

"I figure $25 will do it. With that I'll be able to make enough candles to sell and I can pay you back from the profit."

Twenty-five dollars was not an insignificant amount in our family, whose budget was always stretched pretty tight. But my father smiled and took out his wallet.

"I know you will, Dino," he said, handing me the bills.

I started slowly, making a few candles which I sold. With the profits, I bought more equipment and made more candles. By the end of the third month, I had paid back my father the $25 and acquired about $500 worth of supplies. And I had learned a lot about candle making. I made all kinds of candles, in different shapes and sizes and colors. I would hand-paint them myself— this is from a guy who can hardly draw a stick man. Still, for some reason the candles looked good enough to sell.

Fourteen year old Dino stocking shelves with 'Dino's Candles.'
This, of course, was before Dino cut his hair and
became a Republican.

And sell, sell, sell is exactly what I did. I approached beauty salon and gift shop owners and made my sales pitch—as well as a thirteen-year-old can. To everyone's surprise, "Dino's Candles" was off and running.

By the time I was fifteen, I had a couple thousand dollars' worth of supplies and had sold hundreds of candles to a variety of stores, including Fred Meyer. Then, my attention started to turn elsewhere, to sports, cars, and —surprise, surprise—girls. I stopped making candles and gave all my candle-making supplies to my sister Jessica, who took up candle-making as a hobby.

❧

I learned some valuable lessons in those early enterprises which have helped me time and again in my sales career later in life. Number one: Hard work always pays off. Number two: Don't be afraid. Don't let fear of rejection or fear of failure stop you from even getting started on your path to success. You never know what might happen. People might say "yes" to your sales pitch; the worst that can happen is people will say "no." Even if they do, you're no worse off than you were earlier that day.

Knowing how to work hard and overcoming the fear of rejection at an early age have been two keys to my success in life.

❧

I talk often about working my way through college as a janitor. More than once my wife, Terry, has questioned me about this previous career.

"Where are your professional janitorial skills now?" she wants to know, a not-so-subtle hint that she'd like to see me do a little more industrial-strength cleaning around the house. I think I did enough cleaning for a lifetime during my college years.

Just six months after I entered the glamorous field of graveyard janitorial services, Aetna Building Maintenance placed me as a supervisor on a failing account. I was seventeen, managing a crew of eight, all of whom were older than I—which could either be a recipe for failure or an opportunity for success. It didn't take long for me to realize I had to fire some of my workers—those people who just didn't seem all that interested in working. When the remaining crew realized I was serious about doing the job we were all paid to do, they underwent an immediate attitude adjustment.

But I did more than just clean house (so to speak). I led by example. I made sure I went above and beyond the job requirements, showing my crew that, as the supervisor, I would set the standard I expected all of us to uphold. The dynamics on that crew changed dramatically. We worked hard, making saving that account our mission. And together we did.

After my successful first term as supervisor, the company decided to move me to some of their larger accounts. In one multi-story office building, I found a similar situation to my first supervisory challenge: the crew had some people on it who avoided hard work at all costs. This crew of fourteen had a younger median age than my first crew, and, like me, most were students working part-time. It took awhile, but again, by hiring good workers, establishing high standards, and leading by example, I built a crew we were all proud of.

Once again, the firm moved me to another major account that needed structure and strong leadership. Soon, a pattern emerged: If they needed to solve a difficult on-site management problem, they called me in. I was the fireman, the relief pitcher, the go-to guy when they had a tough situation and needed someone they could count on to solve the problem. I enjoyed that role, and it was one that helped me hone many of the skills I would use in the future.

Even though I worked hard in and out of school, my college years were great years. But the fun ended when my father died my senior year. I took the loss hard. I had been especially close to my dad all my life. When I was a boy, we did almost everything together. In later years, his support and guidance meant everything to me. He was only sixty-one when he died of a heart attack.

Seeing my dad die at a relatively young age made me look at life differently. I figured I'd better live life now, for who knew how long any of us had on this earth. And so I began what I call the "daredevil" era of my life. I rock-climbed with my friend Shawn McDonald, went skydiving with my friend Curt Cleveland. One of my brothers, who had been living in Singapore for a few years, invited me to visit him, so I sold everything I had, jumped on a plane, and made Southeast Asia my home for the next several months.

Traveling throughout Malaysia and Indonesia was the perfect thing for a twenty-something guy to do. Using my brother's apartment in Singapore as a home base, I wandered throughout countries and cultures, taking in a world I'd never known. Talk about a life lesson! I came to realize how we Americans so often take for granted all that we have.

I was in Bali, Indonesia, when it became crystal clear to me how blessed I was to be an American. In a small grocery store, I noticed an odd-looking *Time* magazine on the newsstand. I picked it up and found it was heavy and over an inch thick. When I opened up the magazine, I found a black, tar-like substance covering up certain articles. Evidently, the Indonesian government would only let *Time* magazine be sold in the country if it could censor the articles it deemed "objectionable." That drove home to me the many rights and freedoms we enjoy in our country.

After nine months abroad, I returned to Seattle and the meager $200 in the bank I'd deposited when I was ready to start a new life. Thanks to another brother of mine, I had a car—of sorts.

"It's not very pretty," he said, handing me the title, "and it needs a battery and a starter. But, hey, if you can get it running, it's all yours."

So, I began my adult life with a beat-up Ford, a few bucks in the bank, and nowhere to go but up. I had no real plans for a job, let alone a career. I had a degree in business management from Seattle University, but I knew I didn't want to sit behind a desk all day long. So, like other people looking for work, I turned to the classifieds.

One ad that particularly interested me asked for applicants to become commercial real estate agents. When I met with the sales manager, I found I had one very big drawback.

Graduation day June 6th, 1982. Dino pictured with then president of Seattle University, Father Sullivan

"Kid, you're going to need a real estate license," he said. "I can't do anything for you unless you have that. If you're serious about this business, come back and see me when you've passed the test."

He probably thought that would be the last he'd see of me, but he was wrong. I took the classes, passed my exam, and showed up on his doorstep again.

"What, you're back?" he asked, and, frankly, he didn't look that happy. "You know," he said, "you're kind of young. It's been a long time since our firm has hired someone as young as you. It's hard work, and kids these days don't have what it takes to stick it out."

With the optimism of a twenty-three year old, I assured him I wasn't the kind of person to give up easily. I must have said something right, because I got the job.

Working at this company was like attending the boot camp of commercial real estate: sales meeting every weekday morning, extensive tours of properties three times a week, and long, long hours. They advertised more than any other company in the industry, which was tremendously helpful to someone who didn't have any clients or rich family friends—in other words, someone like me. They housed some of the best commercial real estate agents in the Seattle area.

When I started in 1983, interest rates were at record highs. Competition in the office was stiff. I'd like to say I became an immediate success, but such was not the case. I worked on commission only, and, until I made a sale, I had to survive on beans and crackers. When I got down to that last can of beans in the cupboard, I took a janitorial job at night. But I kept my day job at the real estate company. I would die before I let that sales manager's prediction about me come true.

Fortunately for me, a couple of sales managers and agents took me under their wing, teaching me some of the basics and giving me encouragement. The rest was my just picking up the phone and calling people.

Some people in our office had been there during the boom of the late seventies, when "sales" meant simply answering the phone and taking the order. They still sat and stared at the phone, waiting for it to ring. Well, it wasn't ringing anymore. Agents had to dig up the deals and get the listings through persistence and hard work.

That's what I did. I got on the phone and called the owners of apartment buildings until I found a few who were interested in doing business. By my sixth month in the business, I'd closed three transactions. I thought I was rich! I bought a new car and a few other expensive items before I came down to earth. I suddenly realized that working on a 100 percent commission, with no salary and no benefits, means that if you don't work, you don't eat. That it is truly the free enterprise system, capitalism in its purest form.

I learned another valuable lesson the hard way. You have to manage your money.

Once again I found myself down to my last can of beans. Another three months passed before I closed three more deals. Lesson learned!

A year and a half after I started selling income property, I joined the ranks of apartment building owners. I hadn't planned to, but as so often happens in life, a problem became an opportunity.

I represented a property in the Eastlake area of Seattle, a fashionable neighborhood near Lake Union. This apartment building could best be described as "an ugly duckling." In other words, it seriously lacked curb appeal.

> "Shortly after I was thirty, I owned my first million dollars' worth of real estate."

I showed this property to nine different potential buyers, but I couldn't get anyone to make an offer on it. I explained how a few cosmetic renovations would increase its value.

"But it's lime green," they'd object, wrinkling their noses.

"You could slap on some new paint," I suggested, "and probably increase the income by 20 percent."

In the end, I did such a good job of selling this property, I bought it myself. (Perhaps that's why "they" always say the easiest person to sell to is a salesperson.) I made all the renovations I suggested to my clients and then some. After the remodel, the property increased in value even more than I'd predicted.

Of course, it wasn't easy. I'd used all my available capital to buy the building, having to put the last $2000 of the down payment on a credit card. And at twenty-five, I had never remodeled a building before, and couldn't afford to hire anybody. So I had to learn how to do the work myself. I taught myself to hang sheetrock, change out sinks and faucets, install basic wiring and plumbing, and lay carpet. As my sales business and cash flow grew, I eventually hired people to help. But working on that building was good experience. Not only did I acquire a whole new skill set, I definitely enjoyed a sense of accomplishment when I was done.

That little lime-green building began a new chapter in my business life. I continued to buy properties and shortly after I was thirty, I owned my first million dollars' worth of real estate.

I also learned a lot about human nature in the real estate business. I found I could divide potential purchasers into two general groups. The first group researches each property to its smallest detail. They find and expose all the flaws of a building—and every building has them. They look for reasons *not* to purchase the property. People in this group may buy a building, but it's unlikely.

The second group does the same research and finds the same flaws, but they have a different outlook and philosophy. Instead of using those flaws as excuses to justify their fears, people in the second group figure out how to *overcome* those flaws; they find reasons to buy the property. As you might imagine, individuals in Group Two end up much wealthier than Group One individuals.

The real estate business is a terrific business. It's an equal-opportunity profession, where someone like me, who had no experience, no contacts, nothing to give me a leg up on my competition, could work twelve hours a day, six or seven days a week, and have it pay off. It's the good fortune I found in real estate that allows me to be involved in public service today. It offered a great training ground for my future as an elected official. In my real estate career, I negotiated million-dollar transactions between powerful people and their lawyers. I didn't get paid unless I got the two sides to agree. When I arrived in the state Senate, I was able to put those skills to good use.

❦

As a small businessman, I've often had a difficult time finding a bank that catered to someone like me. I thought that helping small businesses be successful would be a mission most banks would embrace, but I didn't find that to be the attitude of many in the banking industry.

When I heard from a stockbroker friend that he was considering starting a bank based on that philosophy, I immediately jumped on board. We gathered together a few friends—and we started a bank. Our initial fundraising began in 2001, which, as it turned out, wasn't the best time to start such a venture. With the dot-com crash and the terrorist attacks of September 11th, times were uncertain. Most people were holding back on making any new investments.

Still, we forged ahead because we knew there was a need for a bank that would cater to small businesses—in fact, the difficult times may have made that need even greater. Our mission was to help small businesses be successful. If our clients were successful, then the bank couldn't help but be successful.

We opened the doors of Eastside Commercial Bank in the Spring of 2002 in Bellevue, Washington, and those doors are still open. I am truly proud to be one of the cofounders of a bank that is helping small businesses succeed. The bank is growing rapidly, and I look forward to a bright future for it and the people it serves.

⁊⁊

I'm not sure what I'll do next in the business world, but I do know this: If I work hard, persevere, refuse to give in to fear, and lead by example, I will do just fine.

Key Principle:

Becoming Successful in Business Requires Starting Small, Working Hard, Persevering, and Taking Risks

Most things in life are simple. They may be hard, but they are simple. I have known many successful business people and I always find a similar pattern: They started small, often times when they were very young, they work harder than most, they persevere through trials, and they take risks. That seems to be a pretty common recipe for business success.

Of course, most people start small. That is a given. Dino started about as small as you get—golf ball reseller (and didn't take that big of a second step as a candle-maker), but he was off and running on a long and successful career.

After you start, you have to work hard. There is a price to pay for success and it usually means working long, hard hours as you are building your business. Again, most small business people know this. But then there are the final two, and this is usually where you separate the modestly successful from the very successful. The first is perseverance. Trials, struggles, and obstacles will always present themselves. The question that will determine your success is whether or not you will persevere through them. Will you push through or give up?

The second is risk-taking. Risk and reward are companions. Those who take the risks in life are those who get the reward. Those who play it safe limit the reward they receive. That is as close to a universal law as it gets.

How are you living your life? Are you starting small, working hard, persevering, and taking risks? If you want to move to the next level and even further, this is a great roadmap you can follow to get there!

~:Chris Widener

Chapter 3

You Never Fail Until You Stop Trying!

No matter who you are, you are going to suffer a few setbacks in your life. How you deal with those setbacks holds the key to your future success.

Growing up my father always told me, "You never fail until you stop trying."

When I was ten, I loved sports, especially basketball and baseball. I had already achieved some success in baseball, having played on a few different teams. But the basketball I played was mostly playground pick-up games. I'd never played on an "official" basketball team.

One of my neighbors, a kid about my age, was playing on a basketball team whose season had already started. They still had an open slot to fill, and he invited me to come with him and try out. I showed up during one of their practices, and the coach let me play a little bit with the team, then ran me through a few drills.

At the end of the practice, the coach called me over.

"Sorry, son," he said in a voice more gruff than sympathetic, "but you're just not good enough to play on this team."

I was crushed, just crushed—so much so that I had nightmares about it that night. I'd never run into any situation like that before, where I came face-to-face with my inadequacies. I didn't want to tell my parents what had happened. I didn't want anybody to know about my shortcomings on the court. I felt embarrassed and humiliated that I hadn't made the team.

At that point I had a choice. I could let my disappointment in my performance squash my natural love of the game, or I could try to get better. I still loved the game, so I set about improving my skills. I played basketball every opportunity I got. I worked tirelessly on dribbling and shooting and, most importantly, on my defense. After years of practice, I knew I had become a better player, but was I good enough to play on a team?

I learned the answer to that question when, as a student at Mountlake Terrace Junior High, I mustered up enough courage to try out for the basketball team. I knew I might not make the team, but I also knew that wouldn't make me a failure, because of something my dad had drilled into me: You never fail until you stop trying.

I made the team, which had some impressive players. Making that team meant a lot to me. Even though I wasn't one of the best players, through hard work and refusing to give up, I had earned a spot on that team. During my ninth-grade year, our basketball team was terrific—we played together well and had such great talent. A number of my teammates went on to play college basketball. It was something I would never forget.

Through basketball I learned a valuable life lesson on how hard work pays off. We won almost every game, more games than any other team in the district, and were crowned district champions. And I, a kid who hadn't been good enough to play on a basketball team when I was ten, had earned a place on that team.

Why did this youthful setback have a happy ending? *Because I never stopped trying.* According to my father's principles, I hadn't failed, because I hadn't stopped trying. Also, faced with a setback and knowing what had caused it, I laid out a game plan to change my fortune—in this case, to improve my basketball skills through practice. Even the fact that the basketball coach was not as sensitive as he could have been to a ten-year-old boy's feelings helped teach me another lesson—don't let someone else tell you what you're capable of. It was a good lesson to learn early in life, because it made a huge difference in my approach to the many challenges I would face later.

❦

When I took a job in the commercial real estate business, I had no idea what I was getting into. I'd soon find out.

Our firm had dozens of filing cabinets, each one full of file folders. Each file folder contained information on an apartment, office, or retail building in Western Washington. Often the file included the property's history, such as the number of units, the square footage, rental history, and, most importantly, the chain of ownership. Some of the info dated back to the 1920s.

At first, I was clueless as to what to do. Luckily, a couple of the more experienced agents took pity on me—no doubt because I looked so lost.

"See those file cabinets?" they asked. "Why don't you go pull out some of those files and give the owners a call. See if they want to sell their property. Who knows? Maybe you'll hit pay dirt."

Thankful for their interest in me, I took their suggestion. I looked through the files and selected about a hundred different properties whose owner I would call. This is known as "cold calling," and it's one of the main reasons people don't succeed in sales. It's tough.

I picked up the phone and started dialing, rehearsing in my mind what I was going to say when the person answered. I felt very nervous, to say the least. Introducing myself to a complete stranger and asking them if they would trust me—some kid who had no real business experience—to sell their million-dollar piece of real estate seemed like a bold, even brazen move.

I willed myself through the fear and made the first call to the owner of a building over on Alki Point in West Seattle. When a man answered, I introduced myself, identified the firm I represented, and stated the reason for the call. No sooner had I done this than he started yelling at me, calling me obscene names. Now, I'd been called names before, but at least it was by people who had a passing acquaintance with me, which seemed only fair.

After we got through the name-calling part of the program, the man said, "Listen, you *#&$@*#&, if any real estate agents come on my property, I will call the cops and have them arrested for trespassing!" I tried to calm him down and assure him we would do no such thing, but before I could say anything, he hung up on me.

I sat there staring at the phone, kind of shell-shocked, thinking, "Wow! This is going to be a fun business!" One of the more experienced agents, who had a desk next to mine, heard everything because the man had been so loud. The old-timer let a little grin spill over his face.

"Well, at least you got that one out of the way," he said, his tone amused but friendly. "The rest will be downhill from here." Then he tossed off a great piece of advice. "You gotta keep going!"

> "I sat there staring at the phone, kind of shell-shocked."

I got up to get a can of Coke, then I took a walk around the office. Not only was I trying to calm my nerves, I was asking myself whether I'd made the right career move by taking a job in the commercial real estate business. It had been explained to me that sales was a numbers game. If I kept at it, I'd eventually make a sale, and with the size of the commission checks, I needed to close only a few sales each year to make a living.

My dad's voice kept ringing through my head: "You never fail until you stop trying." I sat down and started dialing. The next person was much more pleasant. He had no interest in selling, but at least he wasn't a charm school dropout like the first guy. I called about 150 different people before I finally found somebody who was interested in meeting with me to discuss selling his property.

Our firm had a system, called a "five building concept." You would find five buildings for sale, and you'd get to know everything about that building: the surrounding comparables of sales and rentals, the rent per square foot of similar buildings, the vacancy rate in other buildings in the neighborhood, etc. Your goal was to know those buildings better than the owners knew their own property. You'd then file as many potential buyers past those five buildings as possible. When you sold one of those five buildings, you'd replace it with a new building to sell.

I kept methodically moving through the process and I ended up listing a few different properties just through persistence. In the business of sales, persistence is essential. Salespeople are taught that a "no" is just a stepping stone to "yes." You know the "yes" is out there somewhere, and you just have to persevere to get there.

While you're working to find that "yes," however, you're not earning any salary, receiving any benefits, or enjoying any bonuses based on how hard you've worked. Commercial real estate sales is 100 percent commission. The reward is and should be commensurate with the amount of risk a person takes. This is precisely how the commercial real estate brokerage business works: Large paydays are possible, but difficult to come by.

❧

In my first few transactions, I had worked countless hours to put them together, but they fell apart for one reason or another. Just like that, a month's worth of work would just vanish into thin air without any compensation whatsoever. It was very easy—and even understandable—for someone to get discouraged in that kind of business. I saw hundreds of people come and go during the twenty-plus years I have been involved in the commercial real estate business. Those who survive are the ones who put one foot in front of the other, every day. They see the bigger picture, and can take a long-term perspective. They understand what steps they must take day after day after day to be successful; they don't let themselves be deterred by setbacks or failures along the way.

As Dad would say, "You never fail until you stop trying."

In 1992, six months after my wife Terry and I moved our family from the Magnolia area of Seattle up to the Sammamish Plateau, a suburb east of Seattle, redistricting created a new legislative district in my area with no incumbents. A number of people recruited me to run for the new Senate seat. I was just thirty-two years old, but I was flattered and encouraged that so many people I respected thought I would be a good candidate.

So, I ran. And I lost.

As any candidate will tell you, running for office means putting your heart and soul into the race. I had put my business on hold and dedicated my time and effort to taking my ideas directly to my potential constituents. I personally door-belled thousands and thousands of homes, speaking to voters one at a time, talking about my philosophy, listening to their concerns, and asking for their support. After all that work, investing so much time and effort, to come up 1,051 votes short was hard to take.

Most people who run for office and lose never run again, because it takes such a toll on you and your family. It's one thing to be a volunteer in a campaign; I had wonderful people working with me, and they were terribly disappointed too. But you really never know what it is like to be the candidate until you actually put your name on that yard sign. You're putting your reputation on the line, making yourself vulnerable, waiting for your neighbors and friends to go "thumbs up" or "thumbs down." Getting the "thumbs down" feels like a punch to the solar plexus.

After I lost that election, I spent a couple of weeks at home trying to figure out what went wrong. I was going to stay in the commercial real estate business, of course, but I was still feeling the effects of being rejected by the voters. I moped around the house, licking my wounds and, unfortunately, forgetting some of the lessons I'd learned in life.

Luckily, I am married to a wonderful woman. Terry brought me back to center by suggesting I do two things.

"First, move forward," she advised. "Don't dwell on the negative aspects of losing. Have faith that things will work out."

"Okay," I agreed. "I can do that. What's the other thing?"

"Pray for your enemies," she said, "and for the people who said or did nasty things to you during the campaign."

Pray for your enemies. That was probably one of the hardest lessons I had to learn, but a valuable one. I have witnessed people become bitter and angry because they couldn't let go of the past, and they couldn't forgive their adversaries. Following Terry's advice made a difference in my attitude and gave me the ability to cope with my defeat.

I came to realize that I hadn't really failed, because I wasn't going to stop trying. I would continue to be involved in politics. I began thinking—four years is a long time for my opponent to be in office, to gain a firm foothold in that elected position. In four years I would be challenging an incumbent, and incumbents are harder to beat. I decided that if I were going to win that seat, I'd better start laying the groundwork.

In 1994, when U. S. Senator Slade Gorton ran for re-election, I had the opportunity to chair his campaign in the 5th Legislative District. I worked with a great group of volunteers. For months we worked day and night getting the senator's message out to the voters. That hard work paid off when we won in the 5th district with big numbers—and Senator Gorton won re-election.

The team of supporters I put together was loyal not only to him, but to me as well. If I decided to run again, I had a group of people I felt would likely be helpful and supportive.

When 1996 rolled around, Terry and I decided to "give it another run." Once again, I threw my hat in the political ring, running for the same Washington State senate seat. My opponent was—no surprise—the incumbent, the same person I ran against four years earlier.

But this time around I knew a little bit more about running for public office. My first run had been a good learning experience, because you learn so much more from losing than you ever do from winning. When you win you think you did everything right. When you come up short, you naturally reflect on all the things you did, analyzing what you could have done better. This is true in a political campaign, or in a business transaction, or in everyday family life. We all make mistakes; learning from those mistakes is what allows us to grow.

As I did in the 1992 campaign, in 1996 I hit the streets. Once again, I went door-belling, visiting nearly 15,000 houses personally and wearing out numerous pairs of shoes. Most of the district was located in eastern King County, and much of it was rural. That meant traveling down many a dirt road in search of people who hadn't met me or heard my message.

I remember walking down one such country road when I saw a man coming out of his home. As I made my way toward him, his dog, a little Husky, came bounding out ahead of him. Before I had a chance to defend myself, the dog jumped up and bit me on the hand. As I looked down at an inch-long gash in my hand, blood oozed onto my walking sheet, the document that listed all the names and addresses of registered voters.

The man ran up to me, a horrified look on his face. I didn't miss a beat.

"I'm Dino Rossi," I said, "and I'm running for the state Senate. Do you have any issues at the state level you're concerned about?"

He looked at me incredulously.

"Man, you are committed!" he exclaimed. "You've got my vote. Now, let's go in the house and get that cut cleaned up."

I accepted his offer to bandage my hand. A few minutes later, after thanking the man for his support, I went back to work door-belling.

I knew I needed to be committed and focused, to keep moving forward to accomplish my goals.

Some say defeating an incumbent is difficult, nearly impossible. We ran a terrific campaign in 1996. In some ways, it was a lot easier race, because the incumbent had a voting record—one that didn't match up with what she had said on the campaign trail in 1992.

Our strategy was simple. I compared and contrasted how she had voted with what I wanted to do if I were elected. In the end, I won by a much larger margin than I had lost by four years earlier. I was also the only Republican challenger to beat a Democratic elected incumbent in any race in the state. We Republicans ended up getting the majority in the Washington State Senate.

Victory was sweet and I gave much of the credit for it to my dad. Although he had died several years before, his words lived on: *You never fail until you stop trying.*

Dino being sworn in as a Washington State Senator, January 1997.

Key Principle

Failure Doesn't Have to Be the End of the Road

How many people do you know who, after experiencing a failure, simply gave up? Probably too many. It seems to be the way most people handle failure. But that isn't true for those who become successful in life. In fact, the successful people I know have actually failed more than most people!

Dino has never quit. He didn't quit basketball when he was a child. He didn't quit in those early and difficult days of cold-calling in real estate. He didn't quit after losing his first election. He didn't quit when told his budget would never pass. That is the mark of someone who is successful: They persevere and never quit.

Consider this: When the average person fails, they quit trying, so as to guarantee that they won't fail again (and, of course, they guarantee that they won't succeed either). Successful people, however, keep on trying, in spite of their failure. They learn what they can from the experience and then plug away. They may even fail again and again. Thomas Edison is a great example of this in that he failed a thousand times before developing the light bulb. But he didn't consider it failure. He considered it a lesson on why his invention didn't work, which meant he had one less way he had to try. Eventually he hit pay dirt and changed the way the world lived and worked!

Have you experienced a failure that has caused you to quit or want to quit? If so, now is not the time to quit. Your failure can actually be a stepping-stone experience to a greater success. The key is to not view what happened as a failure, but as a learning experience. When you do that, it will give you the mental focus to try again and make your way to success.

ᴄᴄ:Chris Widener

Chapter 4

HOW TO WORK WITH
THE "OPPOSITION"

As you can see, I put the word "opposition" in quotes in the title of this chapter. There's a reason: I don't really consider people who disagree with me on various issues to be the opposition. I've worked under that assumption my whole life, and I think it's one of the reasons I've enjoyed strong friendships as well as good business relationships. I like to look at people as individuals with whom I can find some common ground.

When I first arrived in the Senate, I looked at things a little differently than many other senators. In politics, some believe that if you don't agree with them on all issues, then you are of no real value. However, I viewed every member of the Senate, no matter how liberal or how conservative, as an individual first. I knew every single member had a value, even if I didn't know where it might be. I figured it was my job find out.

I spent my first couple of years getting to know the senators and many members of the House on a personal level. This was fairly easy to do with my own party, but I also ventured across the aisle to get to know the members on the other side. My goal was to find out who these people were, what made them tick, how they reacted under pressure, and what made them sad, angry, or happy. My reasoning was that I couldn't disagree with a person 100 percent of the time, which meant we must agree at least some of the time.

I was determined to find out just where I could agree with others and when that agreement would make a difference.

Disagreements are not always a bad thing. Debate is one of the great ways we learn both sides of an issue, but it doesn't always have to be adversarial. The key is to be able to disagree without either party feeling as though they're under personal attack.

When you disagree with an opponent—or a friend, for that matter—you never want to burn your bridges. You never know—someday you may need to cross over that bridge again.

$$\maltese$$

Unfortunately, sometimes, it takes a tragedy to make opponents realize the value of overcoming differences to achieve a common goal.

I will never forget one summer's day of 1997 out on the Sammamish Plateau where I live—a beautiful suburban and rural area east of Seattle. I had just finished my first legislative session in the spring, and I remember I was catching up on my "honey-do list" around the house. Suddenly, I heard sirens in the distance, and then closer, and closer still, until I realized they had come to a stop just a few blocks away. Evidently, fire-trucks, ambulances, and the police had all responded. I didn't go investigate, as I never enjoyed watching someone else's misery.

But the next day I found out what had happened. Keith and Mary Johnsen, who lived just down the street from us, were walking hand-in-hand down a road in the neighborhood, a road many of us have walked down with our wives and families on numerous occasions. A van came hurtling down the road, out of control. Before the Johnsens could react, it hit Mary full on, ripping her from Keith's hand. Mary was hit so hard, the impact landed her over a football field's length away from Keith.

Although emergency services responded swiftly, no one could survive that kind of blow. By the end of the day, Keith was a widower with two young boys.

The woman driving the van didn't stop. We found out later it wasn't that she had no compassion for the person she'd hit; she just had no idea she'd even hit someone. Police caught up with her in a grocery store parking lot a few miles away. When they checked her record, they found that she had a number of previous DUI offenses, yet she had never served a day in jail. Not a single day.

When the police gave her a breathalyzer test, she blew over a .30. Most people with that amount of alcohol in their system wouldn't be able to function. But because alcoholics build up a tolerance to alcohol, they can still walk and talk with a higher blood alcohol content.

I immediately received phone calls from members of the local press.

"One of your constituents was killed by a chronic DUI offender," they said. "What are you going to do about it?"

My first reaction was a personal one. "Why me?" I thought. It wasn't that I didn't feel terrible about what had happened to Mary Johnsen. And I felt a deep sympathy for Keith Johnsen and his family. But alcoholism had already brought difficult times into my family.

When I was young, my mother struggled with a drinking problem. She'd go out to the local tavern and come home drunk, which would inevitably lead to a bitter argument between my parents. I was very young, and it hurt to hear my parents argue. I will never forget those nights as I tried to shut out the noise of the two people I loved most yelling at each other.

> "I tried to shut out the noise of the two people I loved most yelling at each other."

Luckily, when I was seven years old, my mother found Alcoholics Anonymous, which changed her life—and our family life—for the better. Not only did she stay sober for the rest of her life, but she founded a number of Alcoholics Anonymous groups which helped other people conquer the disease and control their desire for alcohol. When I was twelve, I went with my mom on what is called a "twelve-step" call, when a member of Alcoholics Anonymous goes to someone in need of help. I remember watching a full-grown man lying on his back, kicking and screaming because he was going through the DTs— delirium tremens—as he suffered alcohol withdrawal. When

people go through the DTs, they sometimes have wild halluci-
nations. This man believed that spiders were crawling through
his veins. He could see them, even feel them. You can imagine
the blood-curdling screams, the violent shaking, the utter ter-
ror of a grown man suffering from such a hallucination.

You would think seeing such a thing when I was young
would have made me steer clear of alcohol. But I didn't. As a
teenager I had a drinking and driving incident myself. Luckily
no one was hurt. After that I believed I could drink and keep it
under control. And I did, in that I never got to the point where I
had to have a drink, and when I did drink, I didn't engage in
reckless behavior. But it wasn't until one morning shortly after
my twenty-fifth birthday, when I woke with one of the worst hang-
overs of my young life, that I had a serious talk with myself.

Thanks to my exposure to alcoholism at a young age, I
understood its power and the devastation it can lead to. I also knew
alcoholism could be hereditary. I figured it would be better for me
to quit while it was still easy, rather than take a chance that alcohol
could get a grip on my life. I knew I didn't want to end up like the
poor man I remembered from my childhood, kicking and screaming and begging for mercy from the torture of the DTs.

So, on October 20, 1984, I said I was never going to drink
alcohol again and haven't had a drink since. Given my background, I think it's one of the best decisions I've made, both for
myself and my family. It's not that I mind if other people have a
drink. Each person is different and knows what is best for them.
In fact, my wife Terry will occasionally enjoy a glass of wine

and, as she likes to say, she had the good fortune to marry a designated driver.

❦

Now you can understand why my first reaction to the Mary Johnsen tragedy was "Oh, Lord, why me?" But, after I actually thought about it, I changed to "Oh, Lord, it has to be me." I understood something about alcoholism. Perhaps I could draw on my difficult memories to do some good.

First I looked at the way we currently handled the problem. Most legislators wanted to be tough on offenders after the tragedy has happened, which included giving offenders long jail sentences. While that might be a fair punishment, it did nothing to prevent the tragedy. I wanted to create legislation that was proactive, rather than reactive.

I started extensively researching legislation, looking at how other communities had handled this problem. I found numerous DUI studies from around the world. Two studies stood out from the rest, one in Maryland and one in Canada, and both involved something called an ignition interlock device. This device registers a person's blood alcohol level. When it's installed on the ignition system of a car, the driver must blow into the device and receive a clear reading before the car will start. The studies found that the recidivism rate—the rate at which people would re-offend—dropped dramatically when this ignition device was installed in DUI offenders' cars.

But this device did more than just prevent drunken people from driving; it collected data. The device housed a computer chip that collected information every time someone tried to start the car. If alcohol was detected in the driver's system and the car failed to start, that was logged in the chip. If someone tried to disarm the device, that action was recorded. Each month the information on the chip was downloaded to the probation officer; a negative read-out could mean a violation of the offender's probation.

One fact I found particularly interesting came from a six-year study in Canada. Research showed the recidivism rate dropped dramatically for offenders who had the ignition interlock in their car on average for only two hundred days. Even though this wasn't a long time to have the device in place, it still had long-lasting effects. Why? Because it broke the habit of drinking and getting behind a wheel of a car.

To me this program sounded so logical. It stopped the drunk driver before the tragedy. I wanted to see our state adopt a similar program.

I sponsored a bill called "The Mary Johnsen Act," the first mandatory ignition interlock law in the country. A driver blowing a .15 or greater on a breathalyzer test on a first offense received the ignition interlock. Why .15? It made sense because chronic alcoholics who are the biggest part of the problem are usually blowing .15 or greater because they have built up such a tolerance to alcohol.

I started laying the groundwork by talking to various legislators about my ideas. Republicans were in the majority in both the House and the Senate, so theoretically I didn't need the support of any of the Democrats to get the legislation I wanted passed out of the Senate. But I wanted to work across party lines on this issue. Who on the other side of the aisle might feel the way I did about this bill? As I skimmed through the résumés of the Democratic senators, one name jumped out at me: Senator Adam Kline from the 37th District, arguably one of the most liberal senators whose district lay within urban Seattle, a city well-known for its liberal leanings. But Senator Kline had been involved with Mothers Against Drunk Drivers in King County, and so I thought he might be interested in my bill.

I approached Senator Kline about signing on as a cosponsor of the Mary Johnsen Act.

"The way I see it," I explained, "chronic alcoholics will drink and drive unless you separate them from their car. It makes sense to stop them before they even get in the car. Punishing people after someone has been killed might satisfy a call for justice, but it doesn't bring a loved one back to life. Our system doesn't help the victims or the offenders, who must carry that guilt and remorse for the rest of their lives. And they'll probably get right back in a car after they've had a few drinks."

Senator Kline and I found common ground on this issue. He liked the idea and thought the bill was not only a prudent, but a proactive move. And so, Senator Rossi, a suburban Republican, and Senator Kline, an urban Democrat, cosponsored the Mary Johnsen Act.

Often legislation that brings about a dramatic change in the law doesn't pass the first time it is proposed. Most people told us, "Odds are this bill won't make it all the way though the process. But at least you're paving the way for the future." However,

I felt strongly that the bill needed to pass that session, and I believed that with both Senator Kline and me as sponsors, it had a good chance. I was selling it in the Republican caucus, and he was doing the same in the Democratic caucus. We delivered a powerful one-two punch in promoting the legislation.

The Mary Johnsen Act passed the Senate, passed the House, and was signed into law by Governor Gary Locke on March 30, 1998. I ended up receiving a national finalist award from Mothers Against Drunk Driving for my work. But the real satisfaction came with the knowledge that our bill would save lives.

I'm proud of the work Senator Kline and I did on the Mary Johnsen Act, and I'm also proud of the way we worked together. We found a way to work across party lines and serve all our constituents by instituting good public policy. Throughout the process, I found Senator Kline to be a man of integrity; I believe he felt the same about me. And even though we probably don't agree on a majority of issues, we did find value in each other.

I try to remember this lesson in every area of my life. Everyone I meet, whether it's in business or politics, in my professional life or personal life, has value. It's my job to find it.

Key Principle

You Can Build a Bridge to Anyone,
Even the "Opposition"

I have always been fascinated by people who burn bridges. It just makes no sense to burn a bridge that you may have to get back over someday! Even more important than not burning bridges is to be proactive and actually *build a bridge* where no bridge was before. If we want to be successful in life, we have to realize that we will have to work with people with whom we may not agree—even people others may call the "opposition."

One of the important things to remember is that the person who is your "opposition" is still a person who has great value. Dino went to the Senate with that in mind and went beyond seeing people as Republican or Democrat, but as people. That allowed him to work with people from the other side when there was a bridge to be built, like in the case of working with Senator Kline after Mary Johnsen was killed by a drunk driver.

Think about people in your life with whom you disagree or don't get along, or whom you consider the "opposition." It may be someone at work, a neighbor, or a family member. Chances are you don't talk much to that person, and there may be a coldness between you.

Now that you have that person in mind, ask yourself what kind of bridge you may be able to build to them. Think about ways that you could both benefit from getting along and work-ing together. There is at least one area in which you can do so. When you have that in mind, plan a time to talk with them and propose that you work together. If that person takes you up on it, you will be on your way to a better place, crossing over that brand new bridge!

~Chris Widener

Chapter 5

VISION FOR A BETTER FUTURE

On the wall in the Senate Republican Caucus room we had a little saying which we tried to live by: "We don't attack people, we attack ideas. We attack ideas with better ideas."

❦

In 2002, the year before I became the chairman of the Senate Ways and Means Committee, I was the committee's ranking member, the lead Republican. But we were in the minority. Majorities mean everything in the legislature, because the majority party decides who chairs the committees and which bills come to the floor for a vote.

As the legislature convened, we faced a $1.5 billion deficit. The Democratic majority had a couple of different options, one of which was to raise taxes. We Republican senators, of course, would oppose that idea. Unfortunately, that's the role the minority party usually plays in this scenario—just sitting in their foxhole and criticizing the majority without offering any solutions of their own. This is a bipartisan practice, meaning both the Republicans and Democrats, whoever is in the minority, engage in foxhole sniping.

Our majority leader challenged the ranking members of each committee to break that nonproductive tradition.

"I want you to come up with a vision for what we would do if Republicans were chairs of our committees," he said.

> "Some Republicans thought this was not only crazy, but a politically dangerous idea."

Some Republicans thought this was not only crazy, but a politically dangerous idea. I, on the other hand, thought it was bold, an invitation to step up and lead when most people would be too afraid.

There is a reason very few solutions are ever offered by the minority. It can be politically risky. Invariably someone won't be as enamored with your ideas as you are, and if your idea fails, you may see it used against you in your next campaign. In my experience, most people don't step up to lead unless they are sure there is some benefit to themselves.

As a budget writer without any power, I knew I had a very big task ahead of me. Still, I was determined to find solutions to the budget problem, then emerge from the foxhole and present those solutions to the public.

Throughout the process, I never attacked people, but I did vigorously attack their ideas, and I attacked them with what I felt were better ideas. I had very little help, but lucky for me it was of the highest caliber. Ryan Moore, a very capable and smart young lawyer, made up my staff of one. Occasionally we'd get some help from the Senate Ways and Means Committee staff, but they spent most of their time working for the majority party assembling the budget. For the most part, Ryan and I were on our own.

Every day we worked to figure out ways to "scrub the budget"—to find savings in state government spending. We found a few good ideas in documents detailing previous attempts to scrub the budget. We also contacted local and national fiscally conservative think tanks for ideas. We brought all of these ideas together and started whittling down the deficit, piece by piece. We made common-sense reductions, much like you do in your own household budget.

Some reductions were simple, such as reducing the number of training conferences and retreats that state employees attended. Some cuts were obvious, as the original expense seemed absurd. For example, for some reason, every agency believed it needed a government liaison—a fancy word for a lobbyist. Try to understand this logic: These agencies took some of your tax dollars to pay for someone to go get more of your tax dollars. In our budget, many of these lobbyists got the axe.

During our research we found examples of documented fraud. One audit performed by the State Auditor's office revealed misuse of funds within the Basic Health Plan of Washington, which provides health services to the poor. This audit revealed that a substantial number of people receiving benefits from the

Basic Health Plan did not qualify; in fact, some people made nearly $100,000 a year. More than 30,000 people had given a phony Social Security number or no Social Security number at all, yet they were still being served. Yet advocates for the Basic Health Plan would come to the legislature every year, asking for more money.

"We don't have enough openings and we're oversubscribed," they would complain. Unfortunately, that's a sound bite that plays well at fundraisers and in the media, but it wasn't quite true. The fact was that people who were entitled to this state program were often denied services, because those who didn't qualify had "beat the system" and used up all the available benefits.

A large reason for this abuse was the lackadaisical approach of the executive branch in ensuring recipients were eligible. The state practice was to re-verify income eligibility of just one in eight recipients a year. If you weren't one of the 12.5 percent that were audited, you were home free. In our budget proposal we included more stringent and more frequent re-verification to ensure services were being provided to those the program was intended to serve.

༃

Lawsuit reform—especially in the area of capping monetary awards that exceed actual economic loss—presented another major issue. The state of Washington is one of four states completely vulnerable to lawsuits. While most states have award caps of $250,000 or less, Washington has no limits. When someone sues the state, they are suing every Washington State taxpayer.

There are times when the state should be held liable for a mistake made, but a policy of no caps on awards is not only beyond the realm of common sense, it is irresponsible to the state's citizens. We were paying more every year in lawsuits than we were spending on the entire state parks network. It's equivalent to over $100 per household every budget cycle. It adds up to over 15,000 new enrollment slots at our universities. I think you get the picture—we are talking about a substantial amount of the public's money.

I looked around the nation for a model system that might help us rein in this problem and still allow people to have the ability to recoup their economic losses when they suffered legitimate damages caused by the state. In Florida I found a process that made sense to me. If you brought a suit against the state, you could bring it to trial and the jury could award you whatever they wanted to. But any amount over $100,000 would have to be taken through the legislature in the form of a bill. Every legislator could decide whether it was worth taking money out of their constituents' pockets to pay for those lawsuits.

For example, when now-Governor Christine Gregoire was attorney general, her office missed a filing date on a lawsuit. It cost the state tens of millions of dollars. If the jury award had come through the legislature, each representative would have had to decide whether missing a filing date was really worth taking money out of the pockets of the people they represent. I think that most legislators would probably say, "No, that's not a good use of monetary resources." I proposed the Florida model, but increased the limit to $1 million, which would still save the taxpayers tens of millions of dollars.

ॐ

Another source of savings is contracting out services to the private sector currently provided by the state. For example, Eastern Washington Community College wanted to contract out one year's worth of janitorial services. They opened up bids to the janitorial firms in the community and found they could save the taxpayers a quarter of a million dollars on a one-year janitorial contract. But the state employees' union sued, and the State Supreme Court ruled in their favor, barring the college from contracting out that service. To support its ruling, the court cited the state law that stipulates that if a state employee has done a particular job in the past, then that job cannot be contracted out to the private sector, no matter how much money it saves the taxpayers. To reduce it to an everyday application, it was illegal to hire anyone other than a state employee to unclog a toilet in a state building. This is why, from my freshman year on in the Senate, I sponsored a bill to remove prohibitions on contracting out services to the private sector. Do we need to contract out everything? Absolutely not! But where it makes sense to do so, we should, as long as it doesn't endanger the health and safety of the public. Anytime you can open up the phone book and find a dozen private firms competing against each other for work, then it makes sense to ask for a bid. This proposal has the potential of saving the taxpayers hundreds of millions of dollars.

ॐ

Dino on the senate floor listening to another debate.

When Ryan and I finally completed our project, we actually found more savings than we needed to balance the budget. We put together a proposal called the "RIGHT APPROACH." Each letter in the word "RIGHT" corresponded to some reduction in the budget. In our proposal we demonstrated that we didn't need to raise taxes or do something that would be fiscally irresponsible to create a workable budget. We presented it to the Ways and Means Committee before the Senate Democrats produced their budget. I invited them to pick it up and run with it; we even said it was fine if they wanted to take credit for it. Unfortunately, the chair of the Ways and Means Committee, Senator Lisa Brown, had zero interest in our ideas.

In spite of her lack of enthusiasm—or perhaps because of it—we presented our suggestions at a press conference. Some Republican members of the legislature thought I was crazy for stepping forward with budget ideas and offering solutions to what they viewed to be the Democrats' problems. They weren't really worried about me, of course; they were worried about being hurt politically in the next campaign. I didn't view the problem as a partisan problem, but a state problem, one that affected the very people we'd been elected to represent. What good did it do to sit in our foxhole and carp at the majority without offering solutions—especially when we had those solutions? Stepping up and leading with our chin made a difference in our attitude. Even though we were in the minority, we acted as if we were in the majority, meaning we took the responsibility for finding workable solutions.

Unfortunately, our ideas never made it into the budget, simply because the Democrats had more votes than we did. The

budget they finally produced was probably one of the most fiscally irresponsible budgets I had ever seen. They didn't raise taxes,
but even though I am not a proponent of raising taxes, at least that
would have been a more straightforward and honest way to balance the budget. Instead, they spent a billion and a half dollars
more than the state was projected to receive in revenues.

Think about that. I don't know about your house, but at my
house when I spend a billion and a half more than I take in, the
next year I have a very bad year. Ironically, the next year the
Republicans won the majority and I became the Ways and Means
chairman—the lucky person left holding their bag of rubbish.

The budget they passed made spending and revenue assump-
tions that clearly were not going to come true. They did something that was so fiscally irresponsible that even our Democratic
state Treasurer called it "borrowing on your house to pay for
your groceries." Like most states, Washington received yearly
payments from the tobacco companies as a result of the tobacco
lawsuit settlement. The yearly settlement payments went into
the health services account to pay for the Basic Health Plan and
health care for the poor. The Democrats decided to sell off future
settlement payments at a deep discount to acquire immediate
cash. They called it securitization of the revenue stream.

Borrowing money by pledging revenue streams is a common practice. The state obligates future revenue streams to build
roads, schools, and general government buildings. As private
citizens, we do this when we borrow money to buy a house
instead of paying all cash the day we move in. In these two
examples, the money borrowed is invested in long-term assets.

When you're done making the payments on your house, you have something to show for your efforts. What was fiscally irresponsible about the Democrats' budget is that it depleted the money going into the health services account to pay for health care for the poor, which created a massive shortfall in the health services account. They took the cents on the dollar they received from selling the revenue stream, $450 million, and plugged it straight into the budget to pay for salaries and paperclips. In other words, instead of borrowing money to acquire long-term assets they borrowed money for short-term expenses. In the end, because the Democrats had the majority, they had the votes to pass their plan through the legislature. Governor Locke signed the budget into law and passed on a big mess to us when we became the majority party the next year.

At the end of the session I was extremely frustrated and disappointed with the outcome. But acting like we were in charge didn't end up as an exercise in futility. In 2003, when I became chairman of the Ways and Means Committee, the "RIGHT APPROACH" effort gave me the confidence I needed to take on a budget nightmare. I knew that we could do an even a better job of coming up with more ideas, because this time I would have not only Ryan, but also fifteen budget analysts and lawyers helping me write the budget. It wouldn't be easy; thanks to the 2002 legislature's fiscal irresponsibility, we would face having to fix the biggest deficit in state history. I was going to need every idea we could possibly find to solve the problem.

But I already held a vision of where we wanted to go. And I had no doubts we would succeed in getting there.

KEY PRINCIPLE

You Need a Vision to Create a Better Future

There is an old proverb that says, "Where there is no vision, the people perish," and it is true. The only way to take yourself, your business, and your family to the next level and beyond is to see in your mind the positive vision that your future can hold for you. If you don't see a positive vision for the future, you will stay right where you are forever.

One of the key things Dino was willing to do was to develop and share a plan for the future, even when he knew he was in the minority. That is the mark of someone who sees his success before it even happens. That is the mark of a leader.

Have you given much thought to your future? Can you imagine how it can get better? Have you taken the time to sit down and think and plan about how to take yourself and the others around you to a better place? If not, now is the time to do so.

Take some time this week to think about the future in the following areas: Your life, your business, and your family. Dream a big dream of what your future can hold. Then take some time to lay out a plan and set some goals for getting there. When you have done that, share those plans and goals with someone who can encourage you to get there. Last, and most important, take action on your new vision.

~Chris Widener

Chapter 6

HELPING OTHER PEOPLE BE SUCCESSFUL

Early in my career in commercial real estate, I worked with Leon Moore, an old-school sales manager who had years of successful selling under his belt. One day he took me aside and taught me a valuable lesson.

"Dino," he said, "when you're working with a client, never worry about how big your commission will be. Your job is to help your clients be successful. If you do your job right, they'll do well. And if they're successful, you will be too."

In fact, Leon told me, that's a good philosophy to live by for most anything you do. Whether it's your political, business, or family life, when you put your efforts into helping others succeed, you can't help but succeed yourself.

I took those words to heart and adopted that policy in my professional and personal lives, proving Leon right every time. When I became a state senator, I brought that philosophy with me. It was a foreign concept to many in the political arena. Often in politics—as in everyday life—people come from a position of self-interest: What's in it for me? What do I get out of it? How am I going to get what I want?

Leon's advice helped me go beyond thinking only of my interests and try to understand the bigger picture. This doesn't mean I think only of others. I still have my dreams and desires, and I work on developing well-defined goals and defining the parameters for accomplishing those goals. However, I've found that no matter where I set the boundaries, I can usually find room to be flexible. That flexibility allows me to accommodate others, to help them realize their dreams or satisfy their passions—in short, to help them be successful.

A funny thing happens when you ask people, "How can I help you be successful?" You disarm them. They relax their natural defenses and they open up. They let you into their world and give you an opportunity to help them be successful. And that success is eventually returned to you.

Of course, you'll find that some people react just the opposite way. Because they're not accustomed to someone else trying to help them, they're suspicious. Their guard goes up, and it takes more time and effort to find out how you can help. But if you are genuine in your offer, and patient in your approach, these people too will come to appreciate your help.

ॐ

As I mentioned in Chapter 3, I lost my first race for state senate in 1992, and in 1994 organized a team of volunteers in my legislative district for U.S. Senator Slade Gorton's re-election campaign.

The 5th Legislative District had about 120,000 residents divided into approximately 160 precincts. My goal was to have a Slade Gorton representative in every single one of those precincts. My staff and I worked day and night to accomplish that goal. Our volunteers—who came to be known as Slade's "5th District Army"—tirelessly knocked on doors, talking to neighbors, friends, relatives, and strangers. The results of their hard work were impressive. Senator Gorton carried the 5th Legislative District with big numbers and won reelection to the US Senate. Justifiably, we were proud of our hard work and a job done well.

What did I gain by helping someone else be successful? I ended up with a group of experienced campaign workers who could help me in my next run for office.

❦

In 1997, my freshman year in the state senate, I decided to use this philosophy as the foundation for how I would represent my constituents. Consequently, I did things a little differently than many of my colleagues. I didn't run around Olympia asking people to do something for me. I kept somewhat of a low profile. I listened and I observed. I watched how the other senators reacted under pressure. I noted how they interacted with each other, how they responded when they encountered anger, opposition, and frustration from their colleagues or constituents. I paid attention to the habits and personalities of the people I had been elected to work with. I took in all this information, knowing it would help me deal effectively with all types of characters in a variety of situations as I represented the good people of the state of Washington.

That first year in the Senate, I served on three committees: Ways and Means (state budget), Energy, Telecommunications and Technology (power, phones, and high-tech issues), and the Natural Resources and Parks Committee, for which I was the vice-chair. One of the first things I did was visit every one of my chairmen and say, "I want to help you be the best chairman you can possibly be. How can I help you accomplish that?" Even though they may have been a little surprised at the question, they welcomed the help. They began by handing me some smaller assignments, things they needed to get done that I could do without compromising my principles. As I had already set the parameters on what I could and could not do comfortably—which were influenced by my long-term goals—I knew how much flexibility I had.

By accomplishing some of these smaller tasks the chairmen delegated to me, I earned their trust. They began to see me as someone they could rely on, because I consistently offered my help, did what I committed to doing, and genuinely tried to help them succeed. When bills I sponsored came up before the Senate—one example is the "Two strikes, you're out" bill that put away child molesters and rapists forever after their second conviction—these bills moved through the system rapidly. Why? Because I had helped other people be successful, and now they naturally wanted to help me in return.

As a rookie vice-chairman of the Natural Resources and Parks committee, I worked closely with two men: my chairman,

*Dino, the Vice-chairman of the Natural Resources and state Parks
Committee, conferring with the chairman, Senator Bob Oke*

a great guy, Senator Bob Oke, a Navy man, and his counterpart in the House, another Republican, Representative Jim Buck, an Army man and West Point graduate. Both of these good men had ideas about which natural resources bills should pass. Senator Oke felt more Senate bills needed to be passed; not surprisingly, Representative Buck believed the Senate should pass more of the House bills he sent over. The situation finally reached an impasse, and it seemed as though no resolution could be found that would allow both men to achieve their objectives. As vice-chair, I made it my personal goal to work with them and facilitate a solution where both Senator Oke and Representative Buck got the legislation they worked for. To do so they both made some compromises along the way, but any compromise necessarily fell within the boundaries of the principles laid out by these two strong-willed, but valuable public servants.

Once again I had followed Leon Moore's advice. Because I did, I was able to help others not only achieve their goals, but also pass legislation that benefited many people in our state.

❦

In 2003, I was appointed and confirmed as the chairman of the Senate Ways and Means Committee, the budget-writing committee for the state of Washington. Facing deficits in the billions of dollars, we were weathering one of the most difficult financial times our state had ever seen. Hallmark doesn't make a sympathy card for such an occasion, but many people stopped by my office to offer condolences on my misfortune in inheriting such a fiscal mess. Although many people appreciated my stepping up to the challenge of trying to solve the budget problem, they flat out said they didn't think the problem could be solved in the way I wanted, which was to keep key programs in place without raising taxes. The only possible solution in most people's minds required a raise in taxes.

Before the session started, I hopped in my car and drove around the state to meet with moderate Democrats and some Republicans in their home towns, where I discussed the scope of the problem. My plan was to help make those legislators successful by inviting them to work with me as part of my problem-solving team. Reactions were varied. Some people wanted a lot, some very little. Some people wanted to yell at me; some said nothing. Some people wanted to be power brokers, while others wanted to be heroes. Some people sensed something big was about to happen and just wanted to be a part of it.

"Many people stopped by my office to offer condolences on my misfortune in inheriting such a fiscal mess."

In each meeting, I clearly laid out my parameters: not raising taxes while still protecting the poor and the vulnerable. These principles reflected my goal—to continue to be a fiscal conservative with a social conscience. I listened to the goals of my fellow legislators, always asking what they felt they needed to succeed. With a $23 billion budget to write, I knew I had a tremendous amount of room to maneuver, and in most cases, the legislators and I found ways to create mutual success.

*Senator Bob Morton from Eastern Washington discussing
a budget point with Dino.*

Two senators in particular stand out in my memory and epitomize the kind of resistance I had to overcome. One senator evidently had decided that what I wanted to do wasn't going to work. When we first met, this senator outlined numerous objections to my proposal. This was not a calm discussion, but a one-sided yelling match. The senator was angry and frustrated and wanted to take it out on someone, and that someone was me.

As tempting as it would have been, I never yelled back. I had learned during the course of my real estate career that successful transactions never come together when the parties yell at each other. I remained calm, listened to all the objections, and wrote them down one at a time. The next day, I came back with workable solutions to the previous day's objections. For my efforts, I got yelled at some more and was presented with a new list of objections. Once again, I calmly wrote them down and promised to come back with answers to those questions.

I kept doing this day after day after day until finally the senator couldn't think of any more objections. It was clear that I had worked in good faith to try and resolve every issue, that I continually found ways we could write a budget that would work for everyone. The senator ended up supporting me and helping me accomplish the goals I set, because I had first helped that senator be successful.

Another senator simply wanted to know "Why should I help you? What's in it for me?" I was faced with figuring out how, with fifty different bills to be written to implement the budget, I could help that self-centered senator be successful. Again, I met several times with this senator, discussing issues and finding ways we could resolve them. Eventually we found common ground that fit within my principles and parameters and still fulfilled the needs of the senator's constituents. I helped that senator be a hero; in return, the senator ended up being incredibly valuable to me in my quest to create a budget that was in line with my philosophy of being fiscally conservative while still having a social conscience.

❦

Helping others be successful has proven to be a winning strategy for me—in all areas of my life. However, there is one important rule to follow when applying this philosophy: You must first set the parameters within which you can work and remain true to your ethics and principles. One you establish these boundaries, you then have the freedom to find flexibility within them. You know exactly how far you can go, what measures you can take without compromising your self-respect and the respect of others. After all, you're the one who has to face yourself in the mirror each morning. And you can do so with pride and satisfaction when you know you've helped others succeed—and helped yourself as well.

KEY PRINCIPLE

The Best Way to Be Successful Is to Help Others Be Successful

One of my favorite quotes comes from the incomparable Zig Ziglar, one of the world's most popular motivational speakers. Zig says that you can get everything you want in life if you help enough other people get what they want out of life. That is one of the greatest success principles I have ever heard, and one that all of us would do well to apply to our lives.

Society teaches us to "look out for Number One," but I find that most successful people I meet are usually others-centered—meaning instead of focusing on what they can do for themselves, they focus on what they can do for others. Given that it's human nature to put self-preservation first, this philosophy might seem counter-intuitive. But the fact is that when we help others, we are really helping ourselves. And the sad fact for many is that because they focus on helping themselves first, they cut themselves off from the success and satisfaction they could enjoy through helping others.

Dino learned these lessons early and has demonstrated this throughout his career. He learned that by helping both sides, he would earn more in his real estate deals. As a senator, he learned that he could accomplish his goals by helping others achieve theirs as well.

What about you? Do you tend to be self-centered or others-centered—or somewhere in between? Wherever you fall on the spectrum, take some time this week to focus on helping others first. In doing so, you will see how pursuing that principle will accelerate your success.

ᴖChris Widener

Chapter 7

TOUGH CHOICES AND OVERCOMING FEAR

One of the distinguishing characteristics of a leader is the ability to make tough choices. And one of the most important choices a good leader will make is to overcome fear.

Whether you aspire to lead in your political life, your business life, or your family life, you will inevitably face fear—fear of making the wrong decision, fear of making people angry with you, fear of retaliation, fear of making a fool of yourself.

Fear is a very normal and often necessary human response to difficult situations. But those who lead understand they must confront their own fears, stand up for what they believe in, and inspire others to follow.

After I first became chairman of the Ways and Means Committee, I found myself facing the daunting task of trying to balance the budget without raising taxes—something no one else in Olympia believed possible. I looked at this gaping canyon of a deficit I had to cross to make the budget work, and I knew I

The 2003 Senate Republican class picture

A gag photo thought up by the green eye shade wearing Senate Ways & Means staff.

would to have to say "no" to a lot of people. I'll admit, I felt a bit nervous—of how difficult a task it would be, of the way people would react to what I did, of possibly losing the Senate seat I'd fought so hard to win.

But I also knew that I wouldn't let my fear override what I knew to be the right thing to do. In a frank discussion I had with our majority leader, I laid out my plans.

"I see where I have to go and what I have to do. But if I follow that path, it's very possible I'll be putting an end to my political life." Before he could offer sympathy or reassurance, I cut him off. "But that's okay. I was happy before I got into politics and I'll be happy after I leave. But while I have this window of opportunity, I want to figure out what's right and just go do it."

That was an incredibly freeing moment for me—neither worrying about getting re-elected nor fearing a backlash against the actions I felt needed to be taken. That clarity and confidence came only by clearly understanding what my personal and political goals and principles were. I knew that, at the end of session, I wanted to be proud of the work I had done, even if it meant I'd earned a one-way ticket back to where I came from.

In January of 2003, fear ran rampant in the state capitol, from legislators to lobbyists to constituency groups. They all feared they were going to lose "their" money in the budget. The news media descended upon me because I was the one who had to make the tough choices on the budget—who was in and who was out. Some of the less supportive Democrats were just waiting for the train wreck they predicted my budget reductions would cause.

My office became something of a revolving door. Every ten minutes, someone new came through the door wanting a piece of the $23 billion budget I and my staff were commissioned to write. The frequency of my appointments almost became a joke.

"Senator, your 9:10 is here."

"Senator, your 9:20 is here."

"Senator, your 9:30 is here."

Everybody knew the schedule was tight and that they had to be concise. Since I had built up relationships with many of these people over the years, most of them knew me well and were able to get right to the point. But they were also very nervous that I was going to cut their program. The governor had already proposed some cuts to important programs, such as those that provided services to many of the disadvantaged, so it was clear no program was exempt.

⁂

Some special interest groups decided to lobby the old-fashioned way. Instead of coming into my office and presenting their case, they took the more dramatic route—bombarding the constituents in my district with TV ads, mailers, and phone calls, each carrying the prediction of the dire consequences my budget reductions would bring. They were trying to bludgeon me into what they wanted me to do, in effect threatening me that if I didn't give them what they wanted, I could kiss my Senate seat good-bye. They must have spent tens of thousands of dollars trying to influence me in this manner—until they finally realized I wasn't concerned about getting re-elected and they actually had to come into my office and have an adult conversation about what they wanted. Because I refused to pander to these groups to ensure my reelection, it truly changed the dialogue of the session.

In looking at the budget, I knew we needed to make distinctions between wants and needs. My wife, Terry, tells the story about how, when we first got married, she would find something she wanted to buy for the apartment. Invariably, I would ask her whether the item was a want or a need. She would look at me and say, "Well, it must be a need because I want it really, really bad." She laughs about it now, because she agrees that that kind of spending didn't work for our household, and it certainly wasn't going to work when I was writing a budget. As representatives of the people of Washington, I felt we needed to fund the core needs of the state government, based on our values as a society, before we even looked at the wants.

But it appeared my principles and those of the Democrats conflicted. The Democrats, who controlled the House, wanted to give unionized government workers raises, and they were perfectly willing to raise taxes to make one of their key special interest groups happy. In fact, the House passed several tax increases even after I told them not to waste their time, because such bills would never get past my gavel. I killed every tax bill they sent me.

The governor, too, made it clear what his principles were when he made his reductions: $13 million that would eliminate job training for developmentally disabled youth; $40 million that would have put mentally ill people on the streets; and $70 million that would have closed nursing homes. The governor had also cut funding drastically for state parks, which meant many of them would have closed. On the other hand, the governor's budget contained no raises for teachers, who were actually due a raise, thanks to an initiative that had passed giving them automatic cost-of-living increases.

One of the most active groups happened to be the very partisan SEIU labor union. Over 500 of them marched around my office with bullhorns chanting my name—and not in a positive way. Singing to the tune of *Frère Jacques*, they chanted, "Dino Rossi, Dino Rossi, cheap and mean, cheap and mean." I suppose they weren't completely off base. Terry has sometimes used the word "cheap" in describing my spending habits. But I prefer the word "frugal"—meaning I try to spend money wisely.

> "They were singing, "Dino Rossi, Dino Rossi, cheap and mean, cheap and mean."

But the second part of their chant, which called me "mean," I took exception to. I was the guy who was going to restore many of the cuts the Democrats were trying to make, money that would fund programs for the ill, elderly, and disabled. I felt this was where taxpayer money should be spent—not on giving raises to the special interest groups who funded many of the Democrats' campaigns. While Democrats often gave lip service to supporting the disadvantaged people in our society, such as the mentally ill, developmentally disabled, and people in nursing homes, these

Senators Dino Rossi, Mike Hewitt and Joseph Zarelli wait for
Gov. Gary Locke to sign the supplemental budget.

were not the people who funded their campaigns. I learned not to listen to what people say, but to watch what they did.

I set about crafting a budget that satisfied my principles, a budget I felt best served all the people in our state. First, we were not going to raise taxes. Washington had one of the highest unemployment rates in the nation. What was the point of asking people for more money when they didn't have it?

Second, we were not going to harm the people most in need, the people whom government truly should be helping. I'm referring to citizens who have difficulty helping themselves—the ill, disabled, and elderly.

Third, while it was pretty clear we didn't have enough room in the budget to give all state employees raises, there were a couple of groups that were long overdue. The first group was the classified public school employees—folks who are often overlooked, but do much to contribute to our public schools. These are the people who pick your children up and take them to them to school, who feed them when they get there, who clean up after them when they go home. If your children have special needs in the classroom, these people act as para-educators, helping teachers in the classroom. These school employees don't make a lot of money for what they do, but our schools benefit greatly from having them on staff. I thought they deserved a raise.

The second group I wanted to give raises to was beginning teachers, because I felt we needed to attract good people to the profession and keep them. In advocating for this pay raise, I came up against the pay scale instituted by the teachers' union, the Washington Education Association (WEA), which awarded raises as a percentage increase based on a on a teacher's current salary. Most teachers with many years of experience were making $60,000 or more per year; beginning teachers earned just $28,000. If a five percent increase was given, that translated to a $3,000 raise for the teachers making the $60,000, but just a $1,400 raise for new teachers. This was hardly fair and equal compensation for people performing the same job and it didn't make sense to me. The budget I eventually produced gave pay raises in the first seven years of teaching. No beginning teacher in our state makes less than $30,000 a year today because of the budget I wrote.

Unfortunately, to make this happen, I had to bypass the WEA because the union leadership didn't agree with me. The teacher's union did not want that raise, which just puzzled me. But the general public understood that we needed to give beginning teachers a raise to attract and keep teachers in the profession.

I often think about my father, an elementary school teacher who taught for over twenty years at Viewlands Elementary School in North Seattle. He raised seven kids on a school teacher's salary, but it wasn't easy. He often said, "If you go into teaching for the money, you better get your head examined." But he felt strongly that teachers should earn enough to raise a family.

My dad could have done anything he wanted to do with his life, but he loved to teach. Because he died just nine months after he retired from teaching, he never got to know how many of his students turned out. But I did. I was fortunate to encounter many of them over the course of my campaign for governor. I would get e-mails at the campaign headquarters asking, "Is your father John Rossi and did he teach at Viewlands Elementary

School?" When I replied that he was the same John Rossi, I'd invariably receive another e-mail relating a long story about how my father had helped that person as a student.

One man told the story of how, during the time he was in my father's sixth grade class, he had some real attitude problems, which caused difficulties at home with his parents and family. My dad worked with him, giving guidance, setting some parameters, and demonstrating how he should act.

"If it weren't for your father," this man said, "who knows what could have happened to me."

I heard similar stories on so many different occasions from people all around the state whom my father had taught. These stories reinforced a principle I already felt strongly about: We need good, dedicated people in our schools; we want to encourage more people to choose the teaching profession; and we should focus on attracting people who love the job, who choose teaching for the right reasons.

Even though we had the biggest deficit in state history, and even though the teachers' union opposed me, I wanted to give the classified employees and beginning teachers a raise. I lost on the raise for classified employees; the House Democrats refused to pass that, because all state employees weren't getting a raise. But I did win on behalf of beginning teachers.

❦

Another budget win was on behalf of families who enjoy our state parks system. I was particularly disturbed by the governor's proposal to cut the funding in state parks. Times were

Five year old Dino on a hike with his father John Rossi.

Dino , age seven, camping with his parents.

*John and Eve Rossi razor clam digging on the Washington coast
(1961). This was a frequent outdoor event for the Rossi family.*

*Dino and his college friend Shawn McDonald on a 5 day backpack
trip across the Olympic mountain range in Western Washington.*

tough, and when times are tough families have fewer options for family vacations. Our family weathered our share of tough times. I remember growing up drinking powdered milk and looking for sales on bread at the Prairie Market, so that we could freeze a few loaves for later. The highlight of our summers was going around the state on camping and fishing trips. Dad had all summer off, so we would go for weeks at a time. Washington has some of the most beautiful state parks in the nation, and the idea of closing any of them under my watch was inconceivable. I was not going to let that happen. I made sure I found enough money in the budget to fully fund the state parks so no state park would close. Period. Camping and fishing trips are terrific, affordable family vacations, and the last thing you'd want to do is put that out of reach for the average Washingtonian.

❧

We had a battle on our hands with higher education. I wanted to make sure that college need grants were funded and that a student need grant was available for all qualified college students in Washington. Unfortunately, the House proposed making need grants available only to students attending state universities. This was a terrible idea. I went to Seattle University, a private Jesuit Catholic university, and I received a state need grant. The House's proposal would have been devastating to students like me. I wouldn't have made it through college without that grant, even though I worked three different jobs to pay for living expenses and part of the tuition. When times are tough, you shouldn't limit the options for higher education. I fought hard on this issue and finally succeeded in ensuring that the grants were available to all in-state higher education students.

❧

Firmly stating my principles helped me develop my goals, which provided the framework for the budget. It allowed me to differentiate between wants and needs, which led me to make sound decisions. How did it turn out? I balanced the budget without raising taxes. I received five awards from the developmentally disabled community for my work on the budget. I received the "Cornerstone Award" from Citizens for Parks and Recreation for keeping the state's parks intact. I received a very high honor from the independent colleges, the "Stanley O. McNaughton Award," for my work on higher education. I also received the "Outstanding Legislator Award" from the National Federation of Independent Business and the first annual "Defender of Liberty Award" from the Evergreen Freedom Foundation.

Receiving these awards reinforced my belief that I had crafted a budget based on sound principles that represented the best interests of all Washington residents, not just a few politically connected groups. I was able to succeed because I overcame my fears: the fear of being disliked, the fear of making some powerful people angry, the fear of losing my job. When you face your fears and stare them down, you enjoy a power and freedom no one can take away from you. You can lead based on what you believe is right. And, in the end, people will not only respect you and follow you, they will thank you.

KEY PRINCIPLE

If You Stay True to Your Values, You Can Make Tough Choices and Conquer Your Fear

Everybody has something that will cause them fear. It may be snakes or spiders, it may be public speaking, or it may be risk-taking. But everybody has something they are afraid of. So it's not actually fear itself, but how you deal with your fear that determines your success in life.

Dino had a tough choice to make. He feared that by making that tough choice, his time as an elected official could be over. But he faced his fear head on, made the tough choice, and ended up accomplishing his goals.

The key to maximum achievement is to face your fears head on and conquer them. And the way you conquer your fears is to know what greater good you will receive if you push through those fears. Let's say, for example, that you fear public speaking. But you also know that learning to do it well will enhance your career in sales. What do you do? You get better at public speaking and do it!

It is always a tough choice to conquer your fears. You will struggle with it intellectually and emotionally; some people even feel the physical effects of being afraid. The great thing is that every time you choose to face your fear and conquer it, you make it easier to do so again the next time. And then you find it is easier to conquer other fears, because you know you can.

Are you facing something today that causes you to be afraid? Let me encourage you to face that fear, make the tough choice, and conquer it!

~:Chris Widener

Chapter 8

YOU ARE ONLY ONE PERSON

Even though you are only one person, your power as a leader can multiply if you are willing to delegate your authority. I have been fortunate to have great people around me to help me achieve my goals—in my career in the real estate business, in my work as a State Senator, and in my campaigns for State Senate and the Governor's office.

In your private business life, you enjoy a measure of control over the people you surround yourself with. In political life, you have very little control in this area. When I was elected state senator, I was thrown together with forty-eight other senators. I hadn't chosen to work with them, and they hadn't chosen me. But we had all chosen to be public servants, and everyone was a leader in their own right.

One of the great public servants in our state whom I had the pleasure of knowing was Joel Pritchard, a former legislator, congressman, and lieutenant governor. I was elected to the state Senate not long before cancer took him from us. Joel became a friend and mentor, and I credit him with giving me three pieces of excellent advice: 1) In politics, if you want a friend, get a dog; 2) If someone offers you a breath mint, take it; and 3) You can get many things accomplished if you let someone else take the credit. All three of these great bits of advice have helped me at some point, but for the purposes of this chapter, we'll focus on the last one.

One of the first things I did when I became the chairman of the Ways and Means Committee was to appoint two vice-chairs, two very competent senators I knew I could rely on: Senator Mike Hewitt from Walla Walla, in Eastern Washington, and Senator Joe Zarelli from Southwest Washington. I gave Senator Zarelli the capital budget. When I did so, I outlined the vision I held and the goals I wanted to achieve, along with clear parameters in which to work. I felt confident in delegating this work to Joe, for I knew him to be a very capable man who would—and could—do what needed to be done.

I remembered in 1999, when the Republican lead on the Ways and Means Committee had me negotiate the capital budget, he didn't bring me in to look at the various pieces of the overall state general fund budget. I had to learn on the fly how the budget pieces fit together, which at first left me scrambling. I didn't want to put Joe and Mike in that position. Who knew what might happen? If I got hit by a bus or, as did happen, I decided to run for another office, I didn't want to leave them in the dark.

Dino and Senator Zarelli on the senate floor waiting to vote.

I brought them in on almost every single detail of the decision-making process, so they could see the whole picture. The resulting benefits were two-fold. First, the Republican Caucus had not just one, but three experienced people who were familiar with all the pieces of the budget. Second, I had two very knowledgeable senators who could defend the budget from the tax-and-spend crowd. In other words, I didn't have to fight all the battles myself.

Along with a budget to pass, we also had fifty different bills to write that were necessary to implement the budget. This was a difficult, time-consuming, and sometimes frustrating process, like putting together the pieces of a jigsaw puzzle. We crafted the fifty different bills, so that together they created a balanced overall budget. If one of these fifty bills didn't pass, it threw the entire budget out of balance. Then we would have to go back to the drawing board to revamp the budget. Given the workload involved, you can see how important it was for me to delegate much of this work.

I did not sponsor most of the fifty bills needed to balance the budget; instead, I delegated them to other senators I knew could take the lead. I set the framework for the necessary work to be done, and the goal I wanted to reach. The senators to whom I delegated tasks would continue to come back and check with me when they made changes in the legislation, especially if those changes affected any of the fiscal amounts. I found it to be a very satisfying process—working as a team to reach the goal of a fiscally responsible budget.

Some people are afraid to delegate tasks, because they think they lose control of the process. But delegating doesn't mean just giving people the authority to do whatever they feel like doing. Successful delegating is set within a specified framework and with clear and established goals based on the delegator's principles.

The following are just a few of the many success stories that came from my delegating to my colleagues:

Senator Don Carlson, who hailed from "Vancouver, USA," as he was fond of saying, was chairman of the Higher Education Committee. I had targeted a few issues I wanted him to tackle head on, which he did in a remarkable fashion. The first issue concerned what I called the "Career Student Bill"; Don ending up dubbing it the "Lingering Student Bill."

State tax dollars are used to subsidize full-time students at public institutions across the state. At the University of Washington the taxpayer subsidy is about $10,000 per student per year. I support this use of tax money, as I believe in giving everyone who wants it the opportunity to go to college. However, I also believe that students can reasonably be expected to earn an undergraduate degree, which typically takes four years, in no more than five years of schooling. I'm not talking about those students who must attend school on a part-time basis due to other obligations, such as work or family, but full-time students who have accumulated more than five years' worth of credits without earning their degree.

Dino and Senator Don Carlson on the senate floor

Unfortunately, too many "career" students were taking up spots in our higher education system. Many were in their sixth, seventh, and eighth year of credit hours earned and had yet to earn that undergraduate degree. I could understand why they weren't in a hurry to leave. Why enter the real world, when being a student was subsidized by the taxpayers?

Not only did I find funding full-time students for an unlimited time to be a ridiculous way to spend our money, I thought it was unfair to all the students waiting to get into college and who had a right to use those state benefits for their own education. Our goal was to write legislation that allowed full-time students to attend a taxpayer-funded state university for five years' worth of credits. Beyond that, the student could still attend that school, but the taxpayers would no longer pay for it.

We saw this bill as a terrific incentive program for full-time students to finish up their degrees within a reasonable timeframe, which would bring about two positive results: One, students would earn their degrees sooner and transition into the workforce, freeing up slots for new students; and two, the state would be able to subsidize more students who wanted to graduate before they were old and gray. Unfortunately, the bill was watered down in the House.

⚜

Senator Linda Parlette, from Wenatchee in Eastern Washington, was an expert in the health care field, and I was fortunate enough to have her on the Ways and Means Committee. She handled many of the tough health care bills for me. Somehow we

Dino and Senator Parlette

had to strike a balance between saving taxpayers' hard-earned money and protecting those truly in need. Unfortunately, the state was broke, and we couldn't afford to add any new spending to fund the programs we wanted to keep.

Senator Parlette helped me stop some of the more outrageous and expensive proposals. She stood strong and fought off bills that would have blown a major hole in the budget. Working with Linda illustrated another benefit of delegating. Because she had forged different relationships than I had, I suddenly had a broader scope of people with whom I could work. I could leverage those extended relationships to achieve our budget goals.

❦

In my time in the Senate, I found two senators who shared my passion for being fiscally conservative, while still protecting the poor and the most vulnerable in our society. Republican Senator Val Stevens and Democrat Senator Jim Hargrove stand out when it comes to protecting our citizens. Some of the most difficult efficiencies that needed to be made in the budget had to come through the Health and Human Services and Corrections Committee, where Senator Stevens was the chair and Senator Hargrove the ranking minority member. I clearly stated that my goal was to protect the vulnerable, the very same people these two senators wanted to protect. But I also wanted to reach that goal staying within the parameters of being fiscally conservative and not raising taxes.

They wrote bill after bill, every one of which required political skill and courage to be an advocate for. I think Senator

Stevens, who had consistently proved to be a good senator, became a great senator, a true leader in the Senate who could take on tough issues, analyze the situation, and present both problem and solution in a concise, coherent way. I believe that sharing the responsibilities of her committee with Senator Hargrove brought out the best in Senator Stevens. These two senators, working together in the spirit of bipartisanship, made a tremendous and positive difference for the state of Washington. Without their help, I don't believe I could have successfully protected the funding for the neediest in our state.

❧

One of the methods I used to create a workable budget was to seek out a philosophical majority, versus a partisan majority, a feat rarely accomplished in politics. But I did achieve that goal on several occasions. One instance in particular came in working with Senator Tim Sheldon, a rural Democrat senator from Potlatch, Washington. We Republicans felt so strongly about his abilities as well as his fiscal and business philosophy that when we won the majority in 2003, we made him the chairman of the Economic Development Committee—something I don't think had ever been done before or since. I served on this committee, so I had the pleasure of watching him use his considerable leadership skills.

Senator Sheldon also impressed me as a man of integrity who always put his constituents first. Together we wrote the economic development budget for the Community, Trade, and Economic Development Department—just the two of us, a Democrat and a

Republican, holed up in a room together, hammering out what needed to be done to write an important portion of the budget. We were able to work together so well thanks to a couple of tenets I always try to follow: Don't burn your bridges and appreciate that each person has a value. Once again, those principles served me well.

֍

So how did we do with the budget in the end? In spite of the scrutiny of the media and constant pessimism from the naysayers, we ended up passing every one of those fifty bills we needed to implement the budget. What I am most proud of, however, is that we succeeded in forming a philosophical majority, rather than a partisan majority. Every one of those fifty bills was passed into law with votes from both parties—not one bill skated through due to partisan politics. People who have worked in the state capitol for as long thirty years said they had never seen anything like that before.

We were able to create that environment of bipartisan cooperation, because we didn't just empower Republicans or those people who agreed with us all the time. We empowered anybody who wanted to work with us. We saw value in Republicans and Democrats alike.

"We had succeeded in forming a philosophical majority, rather than a partisan majority."

I also realized that, being just one person, my skill set and relationships were finite. Allowing others to utilize their talents and connections extended my own scope of what I could accomplish, while helping others be successful individually. This kind of delegation brings everyone into the same boat. Suddenly you're all rowing in the same direction. And because each person can contribute to the common goal, they take ownership of the outcome.

For some, delegating is difficult; they feel they must be involved in every decision, critique every move. But such micromanagement erodes the confidence of others, undermining the very people leaders need if they are to be successful. No one person can do it all. And those who insist they can will certainly find themselves headed down the road to early burnout—and very possibly an early grave.

True leaders build relationships that empower themselves and others. I call this style of leadership "relational leadership," and it has always worked well for me. When I'm able to build a rapport with people early in our relationship, I find it makes them more open and more comfortable in following me and supporting my goals.

Delegating has helped me tremendously in my professional career in commercial real estate as well as my political career. Any leader who plans on succeeding should make delegating a skill they learn to use often—and use well.

In the end, Joel Pritchard was right about the dog, about the breath mints and, most important, about letting other people have the credit.

KEY PRINCIPLE

You Multiply Your Effectiveness by Empowering Others

I have been researching and speaking on leadership and motivation since 1988, so I have seen countless leaders all across America. There are various styles of leaders, and that diversity is healthy. We can't all be the same or lead the same. But while we all have different styles, there are some general guidelines most successful leaders adhere to. One of the most important guidelines most leaders follow is to empower others.

Dino did this right off the bat when he appointed two vice-chairs who were capable leaders. He picked people who had different skill sets and different relationships. He knew that he would be empowering them and thus empowering the process, thereby making success much more likely.

There are many leaders who try to do it all themselves. They can't let go. They have to oversee everything. Unfortunately, this hinders their leadership and keeps them from achieving their goals. The better thing to do is to find good people and empower them to help the organization achieve their common goals.

How do you do this? You find good people. You train them. You share the vision. And then you let them try. Yes, they may fail or stumble at first, but if you have the right people, they will learn from their mistakes and quickly get up a full head of steam.

Then you have multiple people working on fulfilling the dream, rather than just yourself, and that is the key to moving your organization forward.

Whether it is in politics, business, or family life, empower others and you will fast-track your vision!

~Chris Widener

Chapter 9

A POSITIVE ATTITUDE
ALWAYS WINS

Naysayers.

No matter what you do in life, they will always be there. You know who they are—those people who seem to delight in insisting "It can't be done." I've encountered them all my life; no doubt you have too. What I try to remember whenever I face the negativity of a naysayer is that their saying "It can't be done" doesn't make it so.

I remember when I first decided I wanted to go to college. My dad was a Seattle public school teacher and my mother was a beautician. It was all they could do to make ends meet with their family of seven kids, of which I was the youngest. They supported my decision, but made it clear that if I wanted to go to college, it was up to me to make it happen.

I had been earning money ever since I started my golf ball concession at the age of seven, so having to work my way through college was nothing new. I worked at a number of different jobs, mostly performing general labor. I didn't care how difficult of a job I had to do as along as I got paid.

One of the best jobs I had was with a janitorial company where I waxed floors at Seattle's most recognizable landmark, the Space Needle. I worked Wednesday through Monday with only Tuesday nights off. My night would start around 3 a.m. and finish around 8 a.m., just in time for me to make my first class, which started at 9 a.m..

I remember one night after I'd been working about six months for Aetna Janitorial Services, the owner of the company made an impromptu visit. To my surprise, he accused me of using a cleaning product improperly.

I was just seventeen years old and had yet to learn the art of diplomacy. I looked at him in disbelief and said emphatically, "No, I didn't!"

"Yes, you did!"

"No, I didn't! Look, here are the instructions, right on the can."

As we each read the instructions, it was clear to both of us that I was right. Suddenly it occurred to me that maybe this was one of those times in life where being right might be the wrong move. As the boss walked away from me, I thought this could possibly be my last day as a janitor. I didn't want to lose the job, as it paid well and the hours worked with my school schedule. A couple nights later, when I showed up to work, another employee told me the boss was looking for me. With a feeling of dread, I went to find him. I had a good idea what was coming.

But I was wrong. He didn't fire me. Instead he asked me if I wanted to be a supervisor. I guess someone who was willing to stand up to the boss and could follow the instructions on a can of cleaning fluid was management material.

That's when he made me the supervisor of an account the company was on the verge of losing. As I mentioned in Chapter 2, I immediately saw why the account was in jeopardy. My eight-person crew consisted of some unmotivated and disgruntled workers who simply logged in their time without much enthusiasm for their work. All were much older than I was, and a few decided right out of the gate they weren't going to listen to a kid.

I refused to be intimidated. Instead I tackled the job with a lot of energy and a positive attitude, full of faith we were going to save this account. It wasn't easy. I had to make some personnel changes and find people who wanted to work. But eventually the right people came on board and together our team saved that account.

I learned early on in life that having a positive attitude, along with setting clear goals and defining the parameters in which to achieve those goals, are essential to anyone who intends to overcome the naysayers and achieve what sometimes seems to be impossible.

❦

I learned another important attribute in overcoming naysayers from my father: patience. Very few things ever fazed my father. Time and again I saw my father handle an uncomfortable or difficult situation with patience, grace, and dignity. He was a rock. Dad had a couple of sayings that I think are good ones to live by. The first is "Getting worked up isn't going to solve the problem." Remembering this wisdom has helped me keep a cool head during volatile situations. The second is almost a corollary: "Nothing is ever as good or as bad as you think it will be." In other words, let neither your fear nor your enthusiasm get the best of you. I do my best to handle difficult situations like my father did— to stay calm, to reassure people that the sky isn't falling, and to convince them we're moving forward in the right direction.

❦

After returning from my Southeast Asia adventure and starting my career in commercial real estate, the naysayers started putting in their two cents' worth.

"You know, you're not going to make any money in that business," they said.

When people say things like that, I have to wonder whether they're worried that someone else will achieve success where they may have failed. To me, their negativity has the opposite effect of what they might suspect. Whenever I'm told "It can't be done," I use that negativity to motivate me. There is nothing I enjoy more than proving the naysayers wrong.

I took the job in commercial real estate. I kept a positive attitude and a balanced approach, which have been two keys to the good fortune I have enjoyed. During my sixth month in the commercial real estate business, I closed three transactions. I rewarded myself by buying a better car. Within eighteen months, at age twenty-five, I bought my first apartment building. I owned my first million dollars' worth of real estate shortly after my thirtieth birthday. How did I achieve all that? Through faith in myself and a positive attitude, set within a framework of long-term goals.

After I had spent a number of years in the commercial real estate business, numerous people encouraged me to run for public office. I must have fallen on my head hard, because I decided to run for the state Senate in 1992. The naysayers came out in full force.

"You are never going to be a senator."

"You won't ever get elected in this state."

"There's no way you can win."

Once again, I used that negativity to keep me motivated. Unfortunately, in Washington State, 1992 was the year of the Democrat, the year of the woman, the year of pretty much everyone else but Dino. I ended up losing by a margin of 1,051 votes, and, to be honest, it wasn't easy to take. But I always remembered my dad's words: "You never fail until you stop trying."

Four years later, I decided to try again. The naysayers were even more adamant this time. After all, I'd already lost once.

I set out to prove those naysayers wrong. I personally doorbelled 15,000 houses—and was bitten by only four (!) dogs in the process. I ran against the incumbent, the very same person whom I had lost to four years earlier. But this time I won, proving the naysayers wrong. The key to the victory was a positive attitude, patience, and focused hard work. I won because I overcame those negative people one at a time.

The win proved to be historic, because in 1996 I was the only Republican challenger to defeat an elected Democrat incumbent in any state legislative race. Consequently, the Senate Republicans received the majority. Yet even on the heels of this win, I had to listen to naysayers.

"Well, you know you're going to get lost down in Olympia. There are 49 senators and 98 House members. You're just one person. You won't have any power."

I didn't care what they said. I kept a positive attitude, because I know maintaining an optimistic outlook attracts the kind of people you want around you.

By my third year in the Senate, I was the head Republican on the budget-writing Ways and Means Committee and the deputy leader of the Senate. I believe much of my rapid rise in politics is due to my can-do attitude. People saw in me someone who could find the positive in most every situation, who viewed problems simply as challenges that could be overcome, and who was willing to work hard.

❧

In 2003, the Senate Republicans received the majority by a slim one-vote margin. That's when I became chairman of the Senate Ways and Means Committee. The Democrats controlled the House and there was a Democrat in the governor's mansion, so I knew that sticking to my commitment not to raise taxes would be an uphill battle.

Before the legislative session started in January, legislative leaders followed the tradition of participating in an Associated Press forum. The panel included budget writers from both parties. Reporters from TV, radio, and newspapers packed the room and proceeded to pelt us with questions, most of which couldn't be answered because it was too early in the process.

This happened to be a particularly difficult time to be an elected official in our state. As they say, "timing is everything in life," and I had the good timing to become chairman of the Ways and Means Committee during the largest dollar deficit in Washington State history. We had a $2.5 billion hole in the budget. The deficit was going up and our state's economists forecasted that revenues would continue to drop. In other words, we had more money going out than we were taking in.

Although we couldn't give the press much information at that forum, I knew one thing I could tell them with certainty. I stood up in front of this room full of press reporters and made a bold statement.

"We are not going to raise taxes, because I believe doing so would harm the economy and throw more people out of work."

As expected, I was hit with a new barrage of questions. How could Washington keep its social programs in place? Where would the money come from? What was I going to cut?

"With my committee, I plan to do everything I can to protect the most vulnerable people in our society because I believe we can be fiscally conservative and still have a social conscience."

I could hear the naysayers in the room predicting my failure. What I didn't know was that I would find some naysayers within my own staff.

As chairman of the Ways and Means Committee, I had responsibility in most all budgetary areas, including taxing, spending, and pensions. Anything over $50,000 that wasn't transportation-related had to come past my gavel. I had on staff about fifteen lawyers and budget analysts charged with helping me write the $23 billion general budget for the state of Washington and the $2 billion capital budget. Many of my nonpartisan Ways and Means staff had several years of budget-writing experience, and they had seen it all—or at least they thought they had. They clearly thought I was misguided in my optimism.

"I hope you don't have any illusions that any of this stuff is going to pass," my directors advised me.

"Have faith," I said, with a smile. "I believe that together we can solve these problems."

To say they were skeptical is an understatement. Every day of the first week of the session, they kept sitting me down and trying to talk some sense into me.

"Senator," they'd say, "you've got to face facts. Making up the deficit is going to take half tax increases and half spending cuts."

"No, I don't see it that way," I'd insist. "I think we can lick this problem without doing that, but I need your help to do it."

The next day they tried again.

"We're constructing another budget to the one you propose, Senator. It's the 'fallback' budget, what will most likely be the 'go home' budget," they said. "It contains half tax increases and half cuts, which really is the only workable solution."

I remained polite, but firm. "No, I'm not going to raise taxes."

This went on all week long. Finally, on Friday, when they came to give me the same old "half tax increase and half cuts" talk again, I decided I needed to really drive my point home.

"Listen, I don't want anybody talking about raising taxes. I know you're all a bunch of NPR-listening liberals," I said, breaking out into a grin, "but I think you're sufficiently cynical enough to be of service to me."

I wouldn't have made that comment to just anyone. I knew these folks well, having worked with them for years. They didn't take offense at my little jibe; instead, they laughed at what they knew to be a joke. They even threw a few good-natured insults back at me. But they did take me at my word on the issue of raising taxes and never mentioned it again.

> "I know you're all a bunch of NPR-listening liberals, but I think you're sufficiently cynical enough to be of service to me."

I knew I finally had the team on my side.

"Okay," I said, "let's go to work and get this problem fixed."

For the next few weeks, we all worked day and night to achieve our goal. I knew we could do it because this staff was one of the best in Olympia, just an incredibly smart, hard-working, competent group of people. A couple of individuals in particular, my staff coordinator, Randy Hodgins, and budget coordinator, Mike Wills—two great guys and, yes, NPR-listening liberals with a sense of humor—did a great job for me. Surrounding myself with good people has always been one of the keys to my success. Having a positive attitude gave my staff the foundation to accomplish what even they thought was impossible.

❦

For years I'd had supporters urging me to run for governor. When Governor Gary Locke announced he would not run for reelection in 2004, my supporters ratcheted up their appeals. They finally convinced me that the time was right to make that run.

Of course, this time there were a multitude of naysayers, and who could blame them? Our state hadn't elected a Republican governor in twenty-four years. As a state senator I represented only 1/49th of the state. Statewide I had only about 12 percent name recognition when I started my campaign. Any bookie would have agreed that betting on me would be a long shot.

I believed it was time for change, and because of that I believed we could win. I married my positive attitude with sound ideas and started drawing people to our campaign. The race was close, and in the end, I was certified the winner twice. I'll talk more about "the rest of the story" later.

What's important about my gubernatorial run is that my attitude made all the difference. Even though I was a "no-name" candidate, a long shot, and a Republican, I believed we could win. And that belief paid off.

❦

No matter how difficult a problem or how big an obstacle might be in my way, I always believe there is a way around it, through it, over it, or under it. Obstacles aren't what keep you from success; it's your attitude that's going to make or break you. If you believe that you are going to fail, you will most certainly fail. If you believe you're going to succeed, you will attract people with a positive attitude. The combined power of a group's "can-do" spirit gives you and others a great chance to achieve your goals.

That's not to say that you can be completely unrealistic in what you want. I love golf, but I'm pretty sure no matter how optimistic I am, I won't be competing against Tiger Woods any time soon. But I refuse to let others tell me I can't achieve something I believe I can. Sometimes I have to be flexible in my approach, but my positive attitude, along with the help of like-minded people, has served me well.

Having a positive attitude can be likened to having a vision. You know you can succeed and you find ways to do it. Once you have a few successes, you'll suddenly find those naysayers are willing to come along with you. They see how your attitude parlays your vision into a reality.

A positive attitude works wonders in every aspect of your life. Being optimistic in business life will motivate the people around you. Combine that with hard work and clearly stated goals and you have a recipe for success that benefits everyone on your team. People are more than willing to rally around someone who believes they can achieve. A positive attitude is the lynchpin of professional success.

The same goes for your personal life. Every family faces challenges; meeting them with a positive attitude will bring your family together, giving you a better chance at meeting those challenges.

No matter whether you're a janitor or a CEO, a single professional or a stay-at-home parent, a college student or a retiree—having a positive attitude will always pay off.

The best part of Dino's day is talking to children from his district about state government.

Key Principle

Attitude Matters More
than Circumstances

There are a lot of things you can't control in life. You can't control the weather. You can't control how other people live their lives. You can't control the national economy (unless you are the Chairman of the Federal Reserve). But there is one thing that you can control, no matter what is happening around you: your attitude.

You get to choose your attitude. Period. If circumstances are bad, you can still choose to have a positive attitude and see the world through optimistic eyes. The fact is, in every situation, there is someone who will come out ahead—and it's usually the person with the optimistic attitude who sees the possibilities in the negative circumstances.

Dino has encountered naysayers throughout his career in business and politics. They told him he couldn't make money in real estate, couldn't get elected senator, couldn't get the budget passed, and couldn't become governor. But he demonstrated one of the fundamental principles of success: He kept a positive attitude in spite of what others told him he couldn't do.

How is your attitude? Do you tend toward pessimism or optimism? Optimism is so easy to achieve if you try. I define optimism as "the choice to see any situation in a positive way."

Maybe you find yourself right now in a situation that is less than what you'd hoped for. That's okay. Take some time to think about a new way to see your situation. What are some positives that could come from where you are right now? What can you do to make things even better than they were before? When you change your attitude, you change things for yourself and others around you, because your attitude is more important than your circumstances!

~Chris Widener

Chapter 10

THE 80/20 RULE OF LEADERSHIP

Leadership can be broken down into two components: projecting a vision and filling in the details. Of these two, which would you think is more important in inspiring others to follow your lead?

If you answered "vision," you've probably already discovered the 80/20 rule of leadership: 80 percent is selling the vision; 20 percent comes from defining details.

❧

I learned about the 80/20 rule during my college years, when I supervised janitorial crews. As you might suspect, cleaning office buildings isn't the most exciting profession, and motivating the staff was always a challenge. But my crews consistently did a good job. Part of my success came from letting them see the big picture—in other words, by sharing my vision.

For example, I would often get assigned to accounts that were not being serviced well and whose business my company was in danger of losing. My job was to improve the service and save the account. To do that, I needed to motivate people around me, to make them want to join me in solving the problem. I learned how to clearly define our mission, and I invited them to share in that vision, which in most of these cases was saving the account. I found my crew members responded to this kind of leadership, and inevitably they took ownership of what needed to be done.

Once we jelled together as a team with a common goal, filling in the details of the process was easy. Time and again we succeeded in bringing up the level of service and retaining the account. That success didn't come from my spending time on the finer points of cleaning techniques, but from communicating my vision and convincing others to embrace it.

❧

When I worked on the Washington State Senate Ways and Means Committee, I regularly had to deal with details. But I was wise enough to know that most of the people I represented didn't want to hear just a laundry list of details; they just wanted to know the vision. One vision I held when I became chairman of the committee was that I wasn't going to raise taxes, but would still protect the poor and vulnerable. The Democrats controlled the House, we Republicans had only a one-vote majority in the state Senate, and a Democrat occupied the governor's mansion.

We were outnumbered, which is why friend and foe alike predicted that we would be unsuccessful in fulfilling my vision.

In December 2002, just before the session started and as required by the state law, Governor Locke produced a balanced budget. This budget was designed to make him appear to be fiscally conservative. In reality, I don't believe he ever intended to implement that budget. I feel confident in saying this because it contained some horrendous cuts—cuts that hurt the most vulnerable in our society, such as the mentally ill, the developmentally disabled, and the elderly. I believe Governor Locke expected Republican and Democratic legislators alike to run away from his ugly budget with its unacceptable cuts. Once the "fiscally conservative" budget had been condemned by both sides of the aisle, he would produce what was called the "book two budget"—the real budget he wanted to propose, which would be the "increase taxes" budget.

> "This was a high-stakes poker game, and I had to call his bluff."

Why did I think Governor Locke would be more inclined to raise taxes than make cuts? Because that has historically been his style of leadership. In 1993, when Gary Locke was the House Democrat budget writer, he gave us the biggest tax increase in state history. And in 2002, he had signed a fiscally irresponsible budget that directly led to the problems we were currently facing.

With my budget experience from the previous year, I felt confident I could fix the flaws in the governor's budget and still not raise taxes. I didn't want to get the "book two budget," the one I knew would raise taxes, but if we didn't accept this first budget, that's what would happen. This was a high-stakes poker game, and I had to call his bluff.

As the new chairman, I decided I would publicly support his budget. I got my chance when, after the governor officially put out the budget, the press came to me for a comment.

"I think the governor did a great job!" I said. "I agree with him that raising taxes would harm the economy and throw more people out of work. I think he and I might disagree a little on the priorities, but I'd be happy to work with him to solve that problem."

By agreeing with him in public, I had accomplished two things. First, I projected my vision—that of refusing to raise taxes—without going into the details. I thought I could avoid a tax increase and still keep my promise to fund programs for the ill, disabled, and elderly, because I had written a budget the year before that did just that—although the Democratic majority had declined to accept it. Second, my praise of the governor boxed him into a place he didn't want to be. When many of the newspaper editorials also praised his budget, the box was sealed. Much of the rest of the session was centered on keeping the governor from reverting to his tax-and-spend roots.

❦

In January 2003, we still had another six months left in the current budget cycle. The reductions the governor had proposed in his budget wouldn't go into effect until July 2003. Until then, he proposed we make zero reductions. I told my Ways and Means staff to quietly start working on reductions for the remaining six months of the current budget year. This would mean crafting what is known as a "supplemental budget," which alters the remaining portion of a standard two-year budget. My goal was to take as many of the governor's proposed reductions for the two-year budget beginning in July and apply them immediately. If he came out against my idea, he would look foolish by opposing his own proposals. The net effect would be an extra six months' worth of savings and fewer reductions we would need to make in the upcoming two-year budget.

In working on implementing some of the reductions, we found a couple hundred million dollars in savings. Armed with this information, I talked with our majority leader about my idea for a supplemental budget.

"I don't know, Dino," he said. "It's risky at best. If we fail to get enough votes to pass it, we could jeopardize our political strength for the rest of the session."

But I had the confidence that comes with experience.

"I believe we can do it," I said.

He looked at me for a long time, then said, "Dino, I trust your judgment."

Once again, this proved the 80/20 rule. While my staff and I worked out the details to support my claims that we could make effective reductions, I didn't have to explain every line item to the majority leader. He knew my work and saw my vision, and he put his faith in that.

Of course, fear of failure could have stopped everything dead in its tracks. But, as an old sales manager of mine often

Dino on the senate floor selling his vision.

said to us: "Don't be afraid to lose something you don't have." That summed up our position pretty well. At that point in the session, we were outnumbered and had very little to lose.

Now all I had to do was figure out how to convey the message in simple enough terms so the logic was plain for all to see. In other words, I had to work on that 80 percent portion of leadership: selling the vision.

I came up with a simple phrase I thought summed up my vision clearly and logically: "If the reductions in the governor's budget are good enough to enact in July, then they should be good enough to enact right now."

I hit the road, visiting newspaper editorial boards and selling the vision. I made the point that making reductions now would lessen the number of reductions we would need to make in the main two-year budget. I started receiving editorial support from most of the major newspapers. It was difficult for anyone to really poke any holes into the theory because it made sense.

By the time the supplemental budget was ready for a vote, we had bipartisan support. By having both Republican and Democrat senators voting for the budget, it became the "Senate budget" not just the "Senate Republicans' budget." But the budget hit a brick wall when it got to the Democratic-controlled House. It languished in the House Budget Committee for weeks, with no signs of life. However, because no one could mount a credible attack against it, the House leaders were in danger of looking like obstructionists. Eventually, they were forced to pass the budget and send it to the governor for his signature.

Once again, 20 percent details and 80 percent mapping the course and selling the vision was what allowed us to achieve our goal.

❧

This exercise accomplished more than just passing the supplemental budget. We Republicans had just acquired the majority in the Senate, and we didn't fully know what we could accomplish. These first small steps built up our confidence—confidence that we could solve some of these problems, confidence in our ability to find our way out of the fiscal wilderness, confidence that we could work together well. This early success quieted some of the people who doubted whether I was going in the right direction to accomplish our goals. People around me started to understand that the vision was attainable—once they stopped assuming what was impossible and began imagining what was possible. My Ways and Means staff was shocked when the budget passed off the Senate floor and even more shocked when the House passed it. The dynamics in that office changed dramatically. They found a renewed vigor for their job. They were excited to have a boss who could sell the vision. And they started coming up with very creative ideas to help us craft a fiscally responsible budget.

❧

There's an old adage: When you ask a watchmaker what time it is, you don't want him to tell you how to make a watch. That sums up the 80/20 rule. The average person doesn't need or want all those details. They want the big picture, the overall vision. While my staff and I needed to know the details, all we had to convey to others was what was relevant to them.

The foundation for selling your vision is to speak in plain English—nothing fancy, just honest ideas presented in understandable language. Often, elected officials talk "over the heads" of others, because they want to show how smart they are—that they know how to "build the watch." Most people don't want to spend their time on details; they just want to be satisfied that *you* know the details.

I've learned that when you talk over the heads of others, selling your vision is difficult, which means leading effectively is almost impossible. I've found an almost embarrassingly easy exercise for crafting a message that gets my idea across simply and effectively. When I go to the grocery store, I will usually bump into a neighbor. During our conversation, I'll try out a couple of phrases or ideas I'm working on. If I receive a puzzled look, I know I need to go back to the drawing board. If I get a head bobbing up and down in agreement, I take that as a sign I'm on the right track, and I try the same phrase or idea on a couple more people.

What I'm trying to do is reduce a concept that's detailed or complex down to a single sentence or two. If you do that, most people can fully grasp your vision. This is not "dumbing down" the message, but simply streamlining it so busy people get enough information to make a educated decision without having to know every little detail.

Let me give you an example of how I used the grocery store technique to come up with a phrase that proved to be pivotal throughout the 2003 legislative session.

It was clear to me House Democrats wanted to raise taxes—not all of them, but a significant number and most of the people who represented the House leadership. It was also clear the only reason they wanted to raise taxes was to give raises to one of their core constituency groups: unionized government workers. But this would not be the best use of the taxpayers' dollars. By prioritizing spending, I could fund all the basic needs of the state, including restoring those awful cuts Governor Locke had proposed. Raising taxes was unnecessary and would have damaged the state's declining economy even further. As it was, we were consistently one of the states with the highest unemployment rates in the nation.

I had neighbors and friends who were unemployed for the first time in their adult lives. They weren't worried about a raise; they were worried about making the mortgage and feeding the kids. That was the challenge facing the average person in the private sector.

I started thinking about how I could explain this dilemma in a succinct fashion to the public. I wanted people to understand that the only reason we would be raising taxes was to give government employees raises so Democrats could satisfy their constituency base.

It was time to go to the grocery store. As usual, I bumped into a few neighbors and I tried out a few phrases. All I received were some blank stares. I quickly realized I was headed down the wrong path, but I knew what the problem was: My message was too complicated. After a substantial rework, I finally got some heads bobbing up and down in agreement. These were the words that brought home my concept best:

"With Washington having one of the highest unemployment rates in the nation, it just doesn't make sense to me to be raising taxes on people who are unemployed to give raises to people who still have jobs."

On the following Monday I went to Olympia and called a press conference, where I delivered this message. At first, just the Senate Republicans started saying it doesn't make sense to raise taxes on unemployed people to give raises to people who still have jobs. Pretty soon the House Republicans were saying it. Then some Senate Democrats started saying it. Even some of the House Democrats started using my refrain.

My Democratic counterpart, who was in charge of writing the House budget, was quoted by the *Seattle Times* as saying, "We're getting creamed by Rossi!"

Well, flattering as that was, the truth was they weren't really getting creamed by Rossi. I had simply combined the logic of the situation with my vision and stated it in a succinct way the average, nonpolitical person could easily understand.

This approach has been one of the biggest keys to my success as a legislator and a businessman:

I know the details, but I also know how to sell the vision.

Key Principle

Learn When to Cast Vision and When to Share Details

In working with business people through the years, I have found that the average person actually has the vision-versus-details ratio backwards. They spend 80 percent of their energy on the details and 20 percent on the vision. I am convinced this is why we have a shortage of genuinely successful leaders. Successful leaders understand that most of the process of leading is to find and cast the right vision.

First and foremost, if you want to lead, you must have the right vision, so if you don't have a vision for the future, that's the place to start. But once you have found the vision for your business or family, the most important thing you can do is to learn how to share that vision with others. Some things to focus on when thinking about casting a vision are:

- Make it exciting – people won't follow a boring vision or a small dream
- Be clear – make sure that the average person can "get it"
- Be concise – it should be short enough to remember
- Beat the drum – repeat it often, so it becomes your mantra and people hear it over and over again
- Use various means – people hear in different ways so use a variety of ways to communicate the vision

Dino hit it right on the head when he said we need to spend most of our time on the vision rather than the details when communicating our ideas to others. You can imagine how people's eyes would roll back in their heads if they had to review, line by line, the billions of dollars allocated in a budget. They want the vision, not all the details.

If you want to grow in your leadership, do what it takes to begin spending more time developing and casting your vision.

⌣:Chris Widener

Chapter 11

How I Ended Up With a Dog Named Dubya

As adults, we usually forecast our future based upon our experiences in the past. That's certainly reasonable, even prudent in many cases. But the past is not always the perfect predictor we think it is.

Take my Ways and Means staff—a bright and talented group of people, to be sure. When I said we were going to balance the budget without raising taxes and still protect the poor and the vulnerable, they told me, in effect, that I was crazy. They based their opinion upon their many years—in some cases, two decades—of state budget writing experience. In the past, every time the state had a budget shortfall, the deficit was erased half by implementing tax increases and half by reductions in spending. This was the way it had always been done, and to many it seemed to be the only way it could be done.

Think about your business life and your family life and you will find a similar pattern. Most of your thoughts about the future are based upon what you think is possible. The following story illustrates a great lesson on how much greater the possibilities may be than you might think.

☙❦

In the Rossi family, we had had two cats as family pets. Both had passed away, but not from old age, unfortunately. The kids decided they wanted another pet, something with little more staying power, and they knew exactly what they wanted: a dog. Knowing how much time and effort a dog takes, I told them no.

"You guys can't even clean up your own room," I pointed out. "How in the world are you going to look after a dog?"

Week after week went by and they kept at it. Our oldest child, Juliauna, who was thirteen at the time, acted as the ringleader. She'd plan her attacks with the skill of a four-star general. She'd send in the troops—Jake, ten, Joseph, seven, and even little three-year-old Jillian—day and night to pester me about getting a dog.

But I held firm against their tactical maneuvers.

"I'm sorry, but you kids have shown me nothing as far as your being able to accept responsibility," I insisted. "If you want to start demonstrating that you're ready to accept responsibility, you can start by cleaning your rooms—and keeping them that way."

Here was an opportunity to do something positive as a parent, I thought. By holding firm, I was teaching them a valuable lesson about responsibility.

Still, the lesson wasn't working quite like I thought it would. They seemed intent on breaking me down and tried a number of strategies—the most notable one being their leaving pictures of dogs all around the house. Everywhere I turned, I found photos of impish mutts with imploring eyes or appealing puppies cuddling together. And, always, they kept up the barrage of hints—well, they could hardly be called "hints" anymore. My kids made it clear in no uncertain terms: They wanted a dog.

One Saturday morning, they filed into my office, one after another, chanting, "We gotta get a dog, we gotta get a dog, we gotta get a dog." Finally, I'd had enough.

"The only way I'm going to get a dog is if the President of the United States tells me that I should get a dog."

"Look," I said, trying to remain patient, "the only way I'm going to get a dog is if the President of the United States tells me that I should get a dog. Other than that you are going to have to prove to me first that you are responsible enough to have a dog. And right now I just don't see it."

When they had left, I silently congratulated myself.

"What are the odds of the President of the United States telling me I should get a dog?" I thought. "Zero! I'm going to make those kids be responsible, do all those things I've been wanting them to do. Then we'll talk."

What I didn't realize was that Juliauna had listened to every word I said and took my ultimatum seriously.

About five months later, I had to go to Washington, DC, on business. Because it was summertime, Terry and the kids planned to meet me at the end of the week so we could see some of the sights in the nation's capital and visit her brother in Richmond, Virginia.

The day they arrived I had confirmed a White House West Wing Tour for the whole family. The kids were so excited, they could barely contain themselves. As we moved from one impressive room to another, we could feel the gravity of years of world-altering decisions made in that elegant and historical house.

As we stood in front of the Oval Office, I saw Juliauna out of the corner of my eye. I couldn't believe it—she looked like she was trying to get past the velvet rope that blocked the entrance.

"Juliauna!" I said, mortified. "What are you doing?"

She looked at me calmly, apparently unconcerned that she was about to breach White House security.

"You know."

"*I know*?" I asked, in disbelief. "What are you talking about?"

She reached into her purse and pulled out an envelope, holding it up as though doing so would answer all my questions.

"What is that?"

"Dad," she said impatiently, nodding her head in the direction of the president's desk, "you know."

"No, I don't know. What is it?"

"Remember? You told us..."

And then I did know.

"Oh no, no, no, no," I sighed to myself.

Juliauna had written a letter to the President of the United States about the Rossi kids' desire to have a dog. I didn't get to read the letter, but she gave me a rough idea of its contents. It began, "Dear Mr. President: Can you please call my dad and tell him that we should get a dog?" Evidently she went on and on and on about how they could be responsible and do a great job taking care of the dog and how if he could just take a minute out of his busy day to give me a call, they could get a dog.

It ended with a polite request: "P.S.: Please don't call too early because there is a three-hour time difference." I was hoping that, being a dad himself, the president would understand she was just trying to be helpful.

Juliauna had planned to put the letter on the president's desk, not realizing that, had she succeeded, the Secret Service would have swooped down on her, confiscated what they would certainly suspect was a letter bomb, and quickly shown us the door—assuming we weren't held for questioning. Luckily, out tour guide stepped in.

"Is that a letter for the president?" she asked. "Why don't you give it to me, and I'll see that it gets put with his other mail."

Perfect! It would end up in the vat with the other 400,000 letters that arrived that day. I figured I was safe, that I could return to using my parenting—not to mention negotiating—skills to help my children learn some responsibility.

Of course, what I saw as a setback to the "cause," Juliauna saw as a huge step forward toward winning the war. For weeks she bugged me every single day.

"Did HE call yet?"

"Honey, you know, he is the leader of the free world. And he gets thousands and thousands of requests every day. He just

Whitehouse pressroom shortly after Juliauna gave her letter for the president to the White House staff.

can't reply to every one of them. I don't think you should count on it."

But Juliauna remained undaunted.

After we returned from DC, I ran into a reporter from the *Seattle Times*. In talking about the trip, I happened to mention the letter episode. The reporter loved the story.

"Listen, if you hear anything from the president—anything at all—call me immediately," he said.

"Come on, he's not going to call," I said. "He's busy. I'm counting on it!"

Three or four weeks later, after returning from a business trip, I was sorting through the accumulated mail my office had sent over. One envelope caught my eye. It had the White House insignia on it. I didn't find this particularly unusual, as I occasionally received general correspondence from the White House. But this envelope was unsealed and unaddressed. When I looked inside, I found a handwritten note, which read:

"Dear Juliauna: Thank you for your letter and picture. I agree that dogs are good friends. I love Spot and Barney. So, please tell your Dad, I think you should have a dog." It was signed: Best Wishes, George W. Bush.

I'd been Bush-whacked.

Of course, I had to call the reporter back—and that's when things really got crazy. The next day, the dog story appeared on the front page of the *Seattle Times* as well as the front page of *The King County Journal*. Our local NBC affiliate, KING 5, saw the story and sent somebody out. KING 5 is also affiliated with

Sept 4, '03

THE PRESIDENT

Dear Juliauna

Thank you for your letter and picture. I agree that dogs are good friends. I love Spot and Barney. So, please tell your Dad, I think you should have a dog – Best wishes, GWB

The handwritten card from President Bush to Juliauna Rossi.

Cable News Northwest, so the segment played on different stations in three different states. But that wasn't enough. When I turned on the TV the next morning, the story was looping on CNN and CNN Headline News.

I'll admit, I thought it was kind of fun to be part of a feel-good story—until I showed up at my Senate office in Olympia. I was flooded with e-mails from people from all over the country, each one telling me that one and *only* one kind of dog would be perfect for kids. Of course, none of these people agreed on what that breed was.

It didn't really matter to us what kind of dog we got, just as long as it was a good family pet. We went to the Humane Society and looked at several dogs, but one in particular seemed to fit. He was probably part lab and who knows what else, sort of a reddish-brown, and very gentle with the kids. We gave him a presidential pardon and took him home.

Of course, then we had to decide what to call him. Jake and Joseph wanted to name the dog "James Bond"—but they'd also wanted to name their baby sister "James Bond." As we batted around different names, we started talking about how we came to have this dog. After a while, the answer became obvious.

And that's how we came to have our own "Dubya" in the Rossi house.

�❧

During the course of the campaign for governor, President Bush came to Washington State. As part of the greeting committee

Dubya, he isn't a purebred or even pretty,
but the Rossi kids love him.

at a fundraiser held at the Spokane Convention Center, I once again had a chance to chat with him.

The first thing he said to me was "Dino, you are going to win."

Needless to say, I liked his attitude.

His next stop was Seattle. Ordinarily, as the Republican candidate for governor, I would have been there to greet him in my home town, but since I would still be in Spokane, the White House had asked that Juliauna and Terry be my representatives.

What an incredible honor! Juliauna and Terry were going to have a once-in-a-lifetime moment, a memory they could savor for the rest of their lives.

The next afternoon, Air Force One landed at Boeing Field, and Juliauna and Terry were waiting. Juliauna held a picture of Dubya in her hand, and Terry carried a little gift for the president's dogs—a bubble machine whose bubbles smelled like bacon. They stood waiting at the bottom of the stairs; they were calm, they were cool, they were collected. The main door to the cabin opened up and out stepped the president. He smiled and waved to a large group of supporters who stood a ways away behind a tall fence. Then he looked down at Terry and Juliauna, and suddenly their cool demeanor melted.

He strode down the stairs and took Terry's hand.

"Just saw the old man," he said in that warm, personal, Texan way he has. "He's going to win."

Juliauna was so nervous she could hardly talk. Mumbling a few words, she thrust the picture of Dubya in the president's

To Terry Rossi
With best wishes,

President Bush, Juliauna Rossi and Terry Rossi standing next to Air Force One. Juliauna is holding a picture of her dog named Dubya.

Air Force One just landed at Boeing Field in Seattle, Washington.

hand. Terry quickly explained the whole convoluted story about getting the dog, ending with how we had come to name him "Dubya" in the president's honor.

The president looked at Juliauna, his eyes twinkling.

"I'm honored."

Yes, a once-in-a-lifetime moment—and Juliauna deserved it.

✿

So what does this story really teach you? That anything is possible. We don't have to let our past experiences limit our future possibilities.

It never entered Juliauna's head that the president wouldn't respond to her letter. She dreamed big and she expected to achieve those dreams. She didn't let her past experience diminish her power to believe she would succeed.

As adults, with so many past experiences influencing our thinking, we sometimes fail to dream big and move toward those dreams. We believe achieving the dream is impossible, that "it simply can't be done." But just because it hasn't been accomplished in the past doesn't mean that it can't be accomplished in the future. When you believe anything is possible, it is.

Dubya has been a terrific addition to the Rossi household and a great help in teaching my kids responsibility. Joseph and Jillian feed Dubya every day; Juliauna walks him. And Juliauna also gets the not so fun part, cleaning up after Dubya. In the end, we all benefited from the experience and learned a great lesson in life: anything is possible.

As a parent, I learned another lesson: "Beware of what you tell your children just to get them off your back." I'm sure if I would have said, "I'll only get a dog if the Pope tells me to," Juliauna would have gone through our parish priest and we would have received a papal edict. So, in spite of all the parenting skills I've acquired raising my four children, when they question a decision of mine, I find myself falling back on those wise words my parents—and probably yours too—often said:

"Because I said so."

KEY PRINCIPLE

Anything Is Possible

Do you remember when you were a kid and nothing seemed impossible? As part of my "Dare to Dream" speech, I ask the audience what they wanted to be when they grew up. I regularly get people who wanted to be astronauts, movie stars, professional baseball players, firefighters, and train conductors. My favorite one ever was a woman who said, "I wanted to grow up and ride with Roy Rogers!"

When we are kids, nothing seems impossible. Juliauna illustrates this perfectly. Why not just ask the president to tell your dad to get you a dog? Anything is possible, right? Juliauna was still in that stage where she believed whatever she conceived could happen; anything was within the realm of possibility. Every child starts out that way. But then we grow up. People start telling us—and we tell ourselves—that dreams don't come true. And so we give up and forget to dream big dreams. We stop trying for the "impossible."

Often we decide our dreams are impossible to achieve before we even try! We let our past predict our future.

Do you have a dream you have given up on or have failed to try and achieve? Life is too short to not pursue your dreams. Take action this week on something that is "impossible!" You may just find yourself living your dreams!

꒜Chris Widener

Chapter 12

FAMILY, THE GOVERNOR'S RACE, AND THE FUTURE

I was the last one to be convinced I should run for governor. After the 2003 legislative session, I had received awards for what we had done with the budget. People had taken notice. Suddenly, I was hearing the same words from all sorts of different sources: Republican Party activists, radio talk show hosts, and even members of Congress:

"Dino, you really ought to run for governor."

While these words were flattering, I didn't immediately take them to heart. I was looking at my options for 2004 and could see a number of choices before me.

My first option would be not to run for re-election to the state Senate. After seven years serving in the state capitol, I realized it was getting harder on Terry and the kids for me to be away a few months out of the year. My second option was to run for re-election, because I loved my job and particularly enjoyed being the chairman of the Senate Ways and Means Committee.

It's one of the more powerful positions in Olympia, a role that allows a person to really make a difference. Another option was to run for our district's congressional seat. I had spoken to the incumbent, Congresswoman Jennifer Dunn, as well as some of her closest advisors, and it looked like she would not run for re-election, choosing instead to wrap what had been a distinguished political career. Because I represented over 20 percent of her congressional district, I felt that, with some hard work, I would have a good chance of winning that congressional seat. As it turned out, our county sheriff ran for the seat and won. I supported him and I think he's doing a great job.

The final option was to enter the governor's race—in a state that hadn't elected a Republican governor in over two decades.

I looked at the race and assessed my potential opponents. Only two seemed to have any possibility of winning the election.

The first, Ron Sims, held the position of county executive for King County, a Democrat stronghold that holds one-third of the state's population. A dynamic African-American Democrat, Ron would have strong support in his county. The other likely opponent was the most feared and powerful Democrat in our state: Attorney General Christine Gregoire. Newspaper after newspaper referred to her as "the juggernaut" or "the machine," the odds-on favorite and the one candidate any challenger should fear. She'd earned such a reputation by winning statewide re-election three times.

As of August of 2003, I had yet to decide which option I would choose when I attended a fundraiser for President Bush. It was held at the home of Susan and Craig McCaw, the wireless communications pioneer and founder of McCaw Communications. I was among the couple thousand of the McCaws' "closest friends" milling about their backyard. But, I found it to be an exciting and electrically charged day, one reason being I would get my picture taken with the president.

The photo reception line was long, weaving throughout the McCaws' enormous mansion. After waiting more than an hour, I finally made it to the front of the line.

I grasped the outstretched hand of President Bush and said, "Hello, Mr. President, I'm Dino Rossi. I am a state—"

He cut me off right in mid-sentence and looked me straight in the eye.

"Being governor of your state is a lot better than being a legislator," he said.

I was stunned. How could he possibly have time to know and care about my political future? It took me a moment to regroup.

"Well, Mr. President," I said, "I do have four small children, and I'm concerned with what an obligation like that would mean to my family."

President Bush's gaze never left my face.

"You can always find reasons not to do something, but your state is in trouble, and you could be in a position to fix it."

Again, I couldn't believe that President Bush seemed to be acquainted not only with the challenges facing our state, but with my capabilities in dealing with those challenges. While I found his words both encouraging and flattering, a little voice in the back of my head said, "Oh, great, now I have the leader of the free world on my back."

In the end, I promised him I would investigate what kind of impact my being governor would have on Terry and the kids. He shook my hand warmly and sent me on my way.

I started talking to current and former governors about what it was like to raise a family while being governor. I spoke with George Pataki, governor of New York, and then-Governor Leavitt of Utah, as well as former Washington State Governor John Spellman, who was a tremendous help to me in the campaign. Finally, I sat down with another former Washington State Governor, Dan Evans, who raised a young family in the governor's mansion. He was incredibly helpful in the decision-making process. He laid out the situation in plain English.

> "Oh, great, now I have the leader of the free world on my back."

"The parameters are really set by the parents, just like you do now in your own household," he said. "The logistics help. You work across the street from the governor's mansion, so being a part of your family's life is possible."

I became more confident that my first and foremost question—whether my being governor would be right for my family—could be answered in the affirmative.

The next piece of the puzzle was to answer the question: Could I win? I sure wasn't going to do this for sport, and I didn't need the governorship to boost my ego. And, although there certainly are perks that go with being the top official in the state, there were sacrifices that would have to be made too.

I thought long and hard about why I would want to be governor. I love our state, and thanks to my state Senate experience, I knew more than most that our state was in trouble. Based on my success in the Senate, and as chairman of the Ways and Means Committee, I believed that, given the opportunity, I could bring our state out of its economic nosedive. But still I wasn't completely convinced I should run.

In the end, what got me into the race was my wife, Terry, a wise, wonderful woman who has always helped me sort through the tough decisions in life. We sat down and talked it all out: the family issue, the various pros and cons, and what I had to offer as a public servant. In looking at the congressional race, I decided my skills weren't needed there, and I believed moving to Washington, D.C., would be hard on my family. As we discussed all the options, it slowly became clear that being governor of the state was the right choice for my skills and experience.

One of the most galvanizing moments in our discussion came from a simple question Terry asked.

To give some background, one of my nephews had gone into business here in Washington, his home state. However, he gave up that business and moved to Arizona—where he started the very same business. He had found that another state offered much greater opportunity for the small business person. He was one of the first family members to move away from Washington State with no intention of ever coming back—and it was quite a shock.

The question my wife asked me that evening was "What kind of state do you want our children growing up in?" Her follow-up question was "Do you want our children moving away

Dino and Mrs. Cheney watch as Vice President Dick Cheney speaks at a fundraiser

On July 26th, 2004, Vice-President Dick Cheney attends a fundraiser for Dino. Three year old Jillian Rossi's blanket was misplaced and she was not one bit happy about it.

someday because there are better opportunities somewhere else? You are in a position to do something about this. If you are willing to do it, then I am willing to support you 100 percent."

No doubt about it, I'm blessed with a wonderful wife, advisor, and friend.

🕉

Taking that first plunge into the political arena can be a bit frightening. When you decide to run for something this important, you nervously look over your shoulder, wondering if anyone is with you.

And so, I felt some trepidation when it came time to make the formal announcement. In November 2003 we put the word out by e-mail and phone trees to potential supporters, but I really had no idea what kind of a reception I would get.

We chose the Village Theater in Issaquah, Washington, to give the announcement speech. Dave Valle, the former catcher for the Seattle Mariners, was kind enough to introduce me before I walked onstage. When I came out front, I was shocked and humbled. The theater was literally packed with supporters, as well as members of the news media. The rally kicked off our campaign with the right energy, a momentum we carried throughout the entire campaign.

I stepped up to the mike, wondering whether what I had to say would inspire these people to believe in me—Dino Rossi, the grandson of a coal miner and son of a public school teacher, an ordinary guy who had high hopes for our state.

As I began to speak, the crowd quieted.

Three Seattle Seahawks headline a governors race fundraiser. Left to right - MattHasselbeck (quarterback), Dino, Mack Strong (fullback) and Rob Tobeck (center).

Dino with former Seattle Mariner Jay Buhner.

"If you have a dream," I started, "a passion, a desire to do better for yourself, for your family, or for your community, then come with me, because together we are going to make history." The crowd cheered, and I felt energized by their enthusiasm.

And I wasn't wrong in my prediction about our making history. Unfortunately, it wasn't exactly the kind of history I had hoped to make.

❦

We spent a year campaigning, putting in countless fourteen- to sixteen-hour days. I gave over a thousand speeches. We attended over 200 fundraisers, including events with Vice President Cheney, Mayor Rudy Giuliani, numerous governors, Jay Buhner (another former Seattle Mariner), and many Seattle Seahawk players, including Matt Hasselbeck (quarterback), Rob Tobeck (center), and Mack Strong (fullback). We had televised debates and editorial board interviews. It was a lot of hard work— but I was having more fun than I was supposed to have. People could always tell I was enjoying myself, which in turn attracted more people to the campaign. We welcomed anybody to the campaign who wanted to work in good faith to turn Washington State around. This was the same strategy I used as a state senator. We wanted to represent not just Republicans, but anyone who shared our vision, which turned out to encompass people of all political leanings. We had so many prominent Democrats supporting us that they started calling themselves the "Dinocrats." I confess, it made me feel good that what I wanted to do was perceived by so

Dino having a talk with Mayor Rudy Giuliani

*Dino discussing the campaign with
Governor Bill Owens of Colorado*

many as being a nonpartisan approach to make our state better. If nothing else, I take satisfaction in having accomplished that.

On election night, it was clear that the race was going to be close. At one point we were running eight points ahead of the president in our state, and ten points ahead of the GOP senatorial candidate. There were over 160,000 people who voted for John Kerry, but who did not vote for my Democratic opponent, Christine Gregoire. I was not surprised. Many times I had seen cars with John Kerry and Dino Rossi bumper stickers on the back; as we traveled across the state, we saw many front yards that displayed John Kerry signs alongside Dino Rossi signs. When the counting was done, we had won thirty-one out of forty-nine legislative districts, six out of nine congressional districts, and thirty-four out of thirty-nine counties, including Pierce County, home of the city of Tacoma, which hadn't voted for a Republican candidate for governor in forty years. In Snohomish County, just north of Seattle, Republicans hadn't won in twenty years. But we won there too.

After almost three million votes had been cast, I was certified the winner by 261 votes. It was one of the closest elections in American history for a race of this prominence. I was the first Republican governor-elect in twenty-four years.

When the margin of victory is fewer than 2,000 votes, the law in Washington calls for an automatic machine recount. I remember watching then-Attorney General Christine Gregoire, my opponent, on TV, after we had just won by 261 votes. In talking to her supporters with the TV cameras rolling, she said, "I am confident that this election will turn around in the recount."

photo by Corky Trewin

Dino making a point during a debate.

Dino's friend Vince Lombardi III, President Bush and Dino just moments after the president encouraged Dino to run for governor.

I looked at Terry. "She's confident this election will be overturned? Based upon what? What does she know that we don't know?"

King County consistently votes 60 percent Democrat. On nine different occasions during the counts and the recounts of King County votes, they managed to come up with more votes than King County officials originally stated they had received. Even so, when the recount was tallied, we were certified the winner the second time by forty-three votes.

At this point, Christine Gregoire had one option left and that was to have the Democratic Party pay for a hand recount. Unfortunately, this law was put in place back when people didn't trust machines; since then it's been documented that the most accurate count comes from a machine count. Even Democratic election officials across the state were saying that the most accurate count had already been made, that a hand recount could easily result in a flawed outcome.

Our former Secretary of State, Ralph Munro, who was a tremendous help during the campaign and a wonderful public servant, explained how hand recounts could not be as accurate as machine recounts. As he explained it, machines don't get tired and machines don't get distracted.

"On the way home from work tonight," he said, "pick up a ream of paper. Then, perhaps after your family has sat down to dinner, take a handful of sheets off the top of the stack of paper, and pass the remainder of the paper around your dinner table. Ask every person at the table to take several sheets and count each piece of paper. Then count them again. I guarantee you won't come up with same number every time." The fact is, people lose their place, get tired, and become distracted; machines don't. People can even engage in worse mischief. Again, machines don't.

I didn't believe the Democrats would pay for a hand recount, because it would be using a less accurate counting method to overturn one that has proven to be more accurate. As I saw it, and said publicly on TV, if Christine Gregoire were to win the hand recount, all she would have in the end would be a hollow victory and nothing more than an illegitimate governorship.

The usual suspects, the left-wing group Moveon.org and government employee labor unions, came up with the $750,000 necessary to pay for the hand recount. Somehow, King County found votes that had never been counted, and the election flipped by 129 votes in favor of Ms. Gregoire.

Ms. Gregoire immediately claimed victory, but only a minority of people agreed with the outcome. According to the polls, only about a third of the public believed she actually won the election. The majority of the voters in the state—including a large portion of Democrats—believed we did.

As disappointing as it was to lose the election, there was a larger, more important issue at stake. Throughout the process, we kept hearing rumors about problems with ballot counting in King County, along with a number of other irregularities. From all reports, this county, a Democratic stronghold, did not appear to be following its own regulations, much less state law. In Washington, we have thirty-nine counties; thirty-eight of those counties have directly elected county auditors who are accountable to the people. King County is the only county which has a partisan appointee in charge of its Elections Department. For this race, Ron Sims, the county executive and a Democrat, appointed Dean Logan to run King County Records and Elections, which oversaw election processes. Dean Logan was previously a lobbyist for the Washington State Labor Council, whose members put millions of dollars into the campaign of Christine Gregoire.

My campaign team had a hard time getting King County to reconcile their books or even give us accurate data on how their ballots were distributed, how many came back, and who actually voted in the election. In the beginning, King County was downright hostile. Their attitude seemed to be "This is how it has always been. Who are you to question how we do things? Just go away." Given their auditing practices—or lack thereof—this attitude was understandable, but not defensible.

When we didn't go away, their next line of defense was to say that this their process had been "transparent." I had to agree, because we saw what they did and we called them on it. I'm sure they calculated that I wouldn't expose them, as it might be detrimental to my political career. But they miscalculated, because my political career is not the highest priority in my life. Operating from a position of integrity, consistently doing the right thing, and being a person my children can look up to far outweigh any need to attain any political office.

❦

In the state of Washington, the hand count is the final and official count, which meant Ms. Gregoire became the certified winner. The Republican Party had ten days to file an election contest. If you had asked me at that point, "Will the party file the contest?," I would have replied, "Not likely." We knew we were up against a political machine we most likely couldn't overcome.

Had Ms. Gregoire won in a straightforward manner, we would have taken our lumps and gone home. But we couldn't help thinking her victory was manufactured. This wasn't just wishful thinking on our part, but the result of hearing so many stories about election problems, mainly in King County. For example, King County had counted thousands more votes than they could attribute to the actual number of people who had voted. We assumed that a simple and basic standard for any election is that every vote should have a certified voter. We found that hundreds of felons had voted illegally. If their voting rights had not been restored by a court, they did not have a legal right to vote. We found people who had remained politically active and cast their vote—even though they were dead.

Another disturbing fact was that, in a number of King County precincts that were strongly Republican, many of the ballots had somehow gone missing. On the flip side, many precincts where my opponent was strongly supported somehow had more ballots than the number of voters who actually voted.

It was clear to all that we had a problem.

The party leaders and I faced a big decision. My advisors warned me that if I let the party file an election contest, I ran the risk of looking like a sore loser, and my political career would be over. But I knew that if I walked away, the election problems would just be swept under the rug.

So the state party filed an election contest in the state superior court. It had been clearly demonstrated that this election, whether through fraud or mismanagement, was a complete mess. We came forward with action items. First, for Washington State to have a legitimately elected governor, a revote was needed; and second, we had to clean up the election process, especially in King County.

The legal case ended up in Chelan County Court, presided over by Judge John Bridges, who had been appointed by a Democratic governor. We started bringing forward the information to support our case, including new and shocking information we learned from deposing King County election officials.

In King County, all of the precinct election inspectors are Democratic Party activists. On the Friday before the election, King County gave these election inspectors all of the blank ballots to take home with them. Unfortunately, there were no tracking procedures in place. That meant King County had no idea exactly how many blank ballots they had given these partisan election inspectors, nor was there any record of how many ballots they dropped off at the polling places on election day. There was no record of how many blank ballots were left over at the end of election night. To top it off, the county has a "ballot on demand" machine back at King County Records and Elections that prints blank ballots for election workers.

It began to make sense how we ended up with more ballots cast than actual voters.

In 2002 I was an international election inspector for parliamentary elections in Macedonia, a former Soviet satellite state in the Balkans. Representatives from each political party could observe the process from start to finish. No single party member could handle the ballots without the opposition party members being present. They knew how many ballots were printed, how many were used, and how many were left over. I'm sorry to say there was better ballot security in a third world country than we witnessed in King County. Television's *American Idol* has better ballot security than King County.

I don't plan on going through the whole election contest in this chapter. That's probably a subject for another book on another day, but quite frankly, who would believe it? In the end the judge in Chelan County simply was not willing to overturn the election, although he acknowledged the election process in King County was in shambles.

❧

As you can imagine, this was an extremely difficult and frustrating time for me, my family, and all the people who supported me. There were many times during this process when it would have been easy for me to get upset, to yell and scream and rail at the utter unfair and illogical practices we witnessed. And most people said they wouldn't blame me if I did.

But I knew that wasn't the way to go. Terry and I talked about how to handle these difficult times. Our children were watching. The citizens of Washington State were watching. In

Dino pictured as an international election observer meeting with Macedonian political party leaders on the day before the 2002 parliamentary elections.

Election day in Macedonia in a polling place located a short distance from the Kosovo border. Dino is pictured with Muslim election officials in the war torn Albanian section of Macedonia.

the end, the whole nation seemed to be watching. We kept control of our emotions. We relied on the facts to support our case.

We learned that you can handle anything, no matter how difficult, with grace and decorum. And when you do, you earn the respect of others. Because we refused to become bitter and angry, our children didn't feel that way either. They were able to accept the situation, and I was proud of how they handled themselves.

Of course, there were times when something outrageous would happen and even they could see the inequities in the situation. For example, nine different times, King County magically found votes that hadn't been counted. Whenever they did, my opponent's vote tally increased, never mine. Then, just before the trial started, ninety-six uncounted absentee ballots were found, 70 percent of which came from precincts I had won. It's a good bet those ballots would have given me more votes. But, since the election had already been certified, those votes could not be counted.

"Hey, that's not fair!" my kids protested.

"No, that isn't fair," I agreed, "but that's the way life is. Sometimes things are just not fair. So, this year, it looks like the only fair we're going to see is the state fair in Puyallup."

That made them laugh.

In the end, we all learned that even though life isn't fair, life goes on. And, no matter what happens, we can too.

❦

When Terry and I look back upon that year and a half, with all of its ups and downs, we wouldn't have traded any of it. We met so many wonderful people around this state. We inspired and attracted new people to get involved in politics. Almost everyone on my campaign staff was under thirty, and half of them had never been involved in politics before. We brought people together—Republicans, Independents, and Democrats— all working for a common cause: to restore opportunities for success in our state. All in all, it was a tremendous experience and we have no regrets.

So what does the future hold for me? Will I ever run for public office again? A number of people did ask me to run for the U.S. Senate. The White House, the Republican National Committee, and the Senatorial Campaign Committee all wanted me to run against Senator Maria Cantwell. Polling indicated I had an 11- to 12-point lead on the incumbent, even though I wasn't a candidate.

When Senator Elizabeth Dole flew out here to talk to me about the possibility of my running, I told her the same thing I had told everyone else. First, I thought it would be difficult on my family. Being a state senator for seven years, with the capitol just an hour and half away, had been difficult enough. I couldn't imagine being on the other side of the country with a young family back in Washington. At this writing, Juliauna is fourteen; Jake, eleven; Joseph, nine; and little Jillian only four. I want to be around for their growing up, and I wasn't sure how I could overcome that hurdle. Second, what could I accomplish if I won? I wouldn't be in a position to fix my state. I couldn't solve some of the problems I laid out during the course of the campaign in our "Forward Washington" plan. I had discussed these concerns with everyone who encouraged me to run.

Finally, it came to the point where every other potential candidate was refraining from announcing their candidacy until I made a final decision. I made a public statement that, although I was flattered, for the good of my family and for what I think needs to happen in our state, I wouldn't be running for the U.S. Senate. I don't need a political career. Public service is not about carving out a career for yourself—it's about being in the right place at the right time to do something good.

❦

As far as running for governor again, I will make that decision in 2007. I have to see where my family is at that point, and then decide whether what I would have to offer is something that would be beneficial to the state of Washington.

But there is something I think people ought to know about me. The first time I ran for the state Senate, I lost. Four years later I came back and won against the very same person who I had lost to.

My desire to solve the problems of my state hasn't diminished one bit. Only the future will tell in what capacity I can continue to serve Washington State and its people.

KEY PRINCIPLE

Your Family Is What's Most Important

When you lie on your deathbed, chances are your coworkers won't be there. If you are a politician, your voters won't be there. No, it's likely only your family will be there. In the end, it is your family who will stick by you through thick and thin. It is your family who will love and respect you throughout your life. It is your family who walks through it all with you.

If that is true—and it is—then we should remember that we need to take them into consideration first and foremost in how we live our lives and make our decisions. Even if the President of the United States is telling you what he thinks you ought to do, if you have your priorities in order, you will remember to put your family first.

Dino has always put his family as his first priority, even when the highest powers in the land have come calling on him to run for office. Ultimately, he knew that he would only do what was best for his family.

Is that how you are living your life now? Are you putting your family and their needs first? If so, that is fantastic! If not, let me encourage you to take a long-term perspective and refocus yourself around your family and the long-range goals you have. If you do, in the end you will experience one of the great joys in life: having a loving, strong, and supportive family.

~Chris Widener

ABOUT THE AUTHOR

Dino Rossi was twice certified the winner of the 2004
Washington state governor's
race before a third recount
switched the results of the
election by the narrowest of
margins. In a state where
Democratic presidential can-
didate John Kerry won handily, Republican Rossi garnered literally tens of thousands of Democratic and independent votes.
No Republican in Washington State had won the governor's race
since 1980.

Dino appealed to a broad base of voters with his straight
talk on government reform and accountability, jobs and economic
growth, protecting the vulnerable, and the importance of bipartisanship. His popularity continued throughout the aftermath of

the 2004 election, including the election challenge he mounted in state Superior Court due to serious voting irregularities in Washington's largest county, King County. Although Dino was not successful in his election challenge, a majority of Washingtonians continue to believe he received the most votes.

Dino Rossi is a constant voice for seeking out what he calls a philosophical majority *vs.* a partisan majority. He is an experienced businessman and a skilled public servant. He was first elected to the Washington State Senate in 1996. By his third year in the state Senate he was Deputy Leader and the lead Republican on the budget-writing Ways & Means Committee. He was re-elected to his state Senate seat in 2000 with nearly 70 percent of the vote.

While in the state Senate, Dino was a strong leader on budget issues. In 2003, after becoming the Chairman of the Senate Ways & Means Committee, Washington faced the largest dollar deficit in its history. Even though the state House and the Governor's Office were controlled by Democrats, Dino worked across party lines and balanced the budget without raising taxes, while still protecting the most vulnerable and disadvantaged. He received numerous awards for his accomplishment. Dino also worked across the ideological spectrum developing bipartisan strategies on an array of issues. He spearheaded legislation to punish drunk drivers and child abusers. He worked to fund the state's salmon hatcheries. He secured funding for Hispanic/ Latino health clinics, and he championed funding for the developmentally disabled.

Dino Rossi is a successful businessman. He has been in the commercial real estate business for 22 years, and is currently Vice President of Scott Real Estate Investments in Seattle. Dino started in the commercial real estate business with $200 in the bank and a $200 car. A year and a half later he purchased his first apartment building. In addition, he is co-founder of the Eastside Commercial Bank, founded in 2002.

Dino Rossi, a Washington native, learned hard work and strong values from his family while growing up in Mountlake Terrace, Washington. He paid his way through college by working as a janitor. He graduated from Seattle University with a Business degree in 1982. After graduation, he was a regular volunteer with senior centers, the Boys & Girls Club and the Nature Conservancy.

Dino and wife, Terry, live near Seattle, Washington with their four children.

For More Information

Forward ▶ **Books**

To order more books go to:
www.forwardbooks.com

To contact Forward books by mail write to:
Forward Books
15100 SE 38th St., #787
Bellevue WA, 98006

Additional information for Chris Widener:
Chris Widener can be reached for speaking engagements at
www.ChrisWidener.com
or by phone at:
1-800-929-0434